SERVANT OF THE CROWN AND STEWARD OF THE CHURCH

The Career of Philippe of Cahors

T0341892

In the thirteenth century, radical reformers – churchmen, devout laywomen and laymen, and secular rulers – undertook Herculean efforts aimed at the moral reform of society. No principality was more affected by these impulses than France under its king, Louis IX or "Saint Louis." The monarch surrounded himself with gifted, energetic moralists to carry out his efforts. *Servant of the Crown and Steward of the Church* explores the career of one of the most influential of King Louis's reformers, Philippe of Cahors.

Born into a bourgeois family dwelling on the periphery of the medieval kingdom of France, Philippe rose through the ecclesiastical hierarchy to the office of judge. There he came to the attention of royal administrators, who recommended him for the king's service. He ascended rapidly and was eventually entrusted with the royal seal, effectively making him the chancellor of the kingdom, the highest member of the royal administration. Louis IX secured his election as bishop of Évreux in 1269. Using the records of his work in Reims, Paris, and Évreux, William Chester Jordan reconstructs Philippe's career, providing a fascinating portrait of the successes and failures of reform in the thirteenth century.

WILLIAM CHESTER JORDAN is the Dayton-Stockton professor of History at Princeton University.

Medieval Academy Books, No. 117

Servant of the Crown and Steward of the Church

The Career of Philippe of Cahors

William Chester Jordan

Published for the Medieval Academy of America by
University of Toronto Press 2020

University of Toronto Press
Toronto Buffalo London
utorontopress.com
Printed and bound by CPI Group (UK) Ltd, Croydon, CR0 4YY

ISBN 978-1-4875-0691-9 (cloth)   ISBN 978-1-4875-3515-5 (EPUB)
ISBN 978-1-4875-2461-6 (paper)   ISBN 978-1-4875-3514-8 (PDF)

Library and Archives Canada Cataloguing in Publication

Title: Servant of the crown and steward of the church: The career of Philippe of
Cahors / William Chester Jordan.
Names: Jordan, William C., 1948– author.
Series: Medieval Academy books.
Description: Series statement: Medieval Academy books | "Published for the
Medieval Academy of America by University of Toronto Press." |
Includes bibliographical references and index.
Identifiers: Canadiana 20190191805 | ISBN 9781487506919 (hardcover) |
ISBN 9781487524616 (softcover)
Subjects: LCSH: Philippe, of Cahors, approximately 1220–1281. | LCSH:
Bishops – France – Biography. | LCSH: France – History – Louis IX, 1226–1270.
Classification: LCC DC91.6.P45 J67 2020 | DDC 944/.023092–dc23

University of Toronto Press acknowledges the financial assistance to its publishing
program of the Canada Council for the Arts and the Ontario Arts Council, an agency
of the Government of Ontario.

Canada Council **Conseil des Arts**
for the Arts **du Canada**

ONTARIO ARTS COUNCIL
CONSEIL DES ARTS DE L'ONTARIO
an Ontario government agency
un organisme du gouvernement de l'Ontario

Funded by the   Financé par le
Government   gouvernement
of Canada   du Canada

Canadä

In memoriam Thelma Hershey *socrus meae*

CONTENTS

CONTENTS

ACKNOWLEDGMENTS

I thank the staff of the Archives Départementales of the Eure in Évreux, who managed to explain to me the computerized retrieval system employed at the collection, albeit I never became very efficient at using it. Even though the spring floods in northern France in 2016 caused damage at the archive, I was warmly greeted by the no-doubt-stressed staff during my first visit in July of that year. The hours for using the archives were severely curtailed by the time I made my second visit there (June 2018), but, once again, the staff was helpful and cheerful with all the patrons. I want to acknowledge also that quite early on in this project Anne Lester discussed several of my arguments with me. The parts of the finished work that benefitted most from her comments will appear separately in the *Festschrift for Elizabeth A.R. Brown* edited by Cecilia Gaposchkin and Jay Rubenstein, but they are summarized in the present book. Another section of this book draws on a plenary lecture I delivered at the annual meeting of the Haskins Society at the University of North Carolina, Chapel Hill, on 27 October 2018. The feedback from members of the audience during the following reception in Hyde Hall's Incubator Room (so named because it is dedicated to the incubation of ideas) was valuable in improving the forthcoming version in the *Haskins Society Journal*.

A word on the dedication: during the last decade of her long life, my centenarian mother-in-law, Thelma Hershey, received a weekly letter from me in the regular post. Men and women of her generation, of whom there are so few still with us, often preferred receiving information in this form rather than as emails, let alone as texts or tweets, even if they acknowledged the value of some of the newer technology, as she certainly did. For me the letters were an opportunity to sum up the week's experiences, to share some of my personal and professional concerns, as department chair for nine years in particular, and to explain what I was trying to accomplish in my research and writing.

I discovered that the effort to do the last of these was extremely valuable in honing my ideas and, indeed, in making them clearer and helping me to identify contradictions and infelicities of expression that I had not noticed working simply on my own. Thelma always seemed to enjoy both my no-holds-barred "evaluations" of departmental colleagues and university personnel and my descriptions, more restrained in tone, of my scholarly work. I was surprised and felt a certain dismay when I learned that she was retaining all the letters – in so great a part, a very choleric archive – in thickly packed three-ring notebooks, numbering by the end in the dozens. (I now better understand the impulse to have one's papers burned.)

Thelma Hershey passed away in the early stage of the writing of this book, and I have sorely missed those weekly opportunities to share my venom and pleasures, a habit that became a kind of periodic catharsis. Early in my acquaintance, I discovered that she loved Latin, which she studied in school, and so I pay homage to her in the words of the poet: *Eheu fugaces labuntur anni* (Alas, the fleeting years pass by; Horace, *Odes*, 2.14).

CONVENTIONS

Unless otherwise noted, all the currency mentioned in this book is French *livres*, *sous*, and *deniers*, abbreviated l., s., and d., but sometimes referred to by the English translations "pounds," "shillings," and "pence." The names of well-known personages, like kings, are rendered in English, so "Philip Augustus" rather than "Philippe Auguste." Most personal names, however, appear in their medieval forms (or modern French forms, if these exist). Exceptions are those names given in the original sources in medieval Latin that do not have post-medieval French equivalents. In such cases, I retain the Latin. The same is true of place names, for some are simply not identifiable in modern gazetteers or similar reference books. If a personal name has a toponymic element, I use "de" if the person under discussion was born to a knightly family or one above that in rank. I use "of" for all others, even if they achieved high government or ecclesiastical posts in the course of their lives. Thus, the mid-thirteenth-century abbot of Saint-Denis appears in these pages as Mathieu *of* Vendôme; his partner as co-regent of the kingdom in 1270 and 1285, the lord of Clermont, appears as Simon *de* Nesle.

CONVENTIONS

SERVANT OF THE CROWN AND STEWARD OF THE CHURCH

The Career of Philippe of Cahors

1

THE EARLY YEARS

No one knew how long it would take to collect testimony on the life and miracles of the French king, Louis IX, when three papal commissioners with their scribes and personal attendants arrived at the royal abbey of Saint-Denis in May 1282.[1] They came to hear and record the words of family and friends and to verify the stories of those healed by the reputed holy man. After a reign of forty-four years, 1226–70, the king had succumbed to disease while on crusade in Tunis.[2] Those accompanying the funeral cortege that brought his bones back for burial in Saint-Denis received reports as they proceeded up the Italian peninsula of marvellous cures and interventions attributed to the king in the localities through which his relics and his mourners travelled.[3] Monks of Saint-Denis wrote memoranda of many other miracles that took place while the cortege processed through France and then afterward, following the king's entombment at the abbey.[4] On 23 December 1281, eleven years after the miracles began, Pope Martin IV authorized a commission to inquire into the French king's virtues in confident anticipation of his canonization.[5] The commissioners' work at Saint-Denis was the direct consequence of the pope's order.

Among those giving depositions on Louis IX's life were many churchmen who had served him in sensitive positions, a remarkable group of advisors and pastors who shared his enthusiasm to establish a holy realm.[6] In talking of the king, they spoke often of themselves, and from their reminiscences, one may

---

1 Carolus-Barré, *Le procès de canonisation de saint Louis*, p. 21.
2 Hélary, *La dernière croisade*, pp. 7–10.
3 Jordan, *Louis IX and the Challenge of the Crusade*, p. 182.
4 Carolus-Barré, *Le procès de canonisation de saint Louis*.
5 Kay, "Episcopal Petition," p. 304 no. 15.
6 Carolus-Barré, *Le procès de canonisation de saint Louis*, pp. 26–7.

piece together telling biographical vignettes of the men.[7] Among the depo-
nents, for example, was Mathieu of Vendôme, the abbot of Saint-Denis, whom
Louis had designated co-regent of the kingdom as part of his preparations for
making holy war in North Africa in 1270.[8] Absent, however – and not because
of a defect in the surviving evidence, but for a much more mundane reason –
was a certain Philippe of Cahors, the bishop of the Norman see of Évreux. He
had died in August 1281, only a few months before the commissioners arrived
at Saint-Denis to interrogate the witnesses to the king's holiness.[9]

There is much that Philippe, who was born about 1220 or a little before,
could have told them had he lived, for he had been very close to the king,
and Louis favoured him to a degree he favoured few other men. The future
saint had stipulated that if Mathieu of Vendôme died in office while he was on
crusade, Philippe was to assume the vacant co-regency – high trust, indeed –
serving alongside the lay lord, Simon de Nesle, whom Louis had designated.[10] Undoubtedly much of what Geoffroy of Beaulieu, the king's confessor,
wrote up in his biography of the king, just as in the book of another close
friend, Guillaume of Chartres, must have assimilated Philippe's memories and
insights, although it is difficult to disaggregate the various voices of writers
and informants. Yet it is possible, as legend has it, that these two Dominicans
(Geoffroy and Guillaume) retired after a long life of service to the royal family
to Évreux, while Philippe of Cahors was still alive and occupied the episcopal throne in the Norman city.[11] If so, it was a very special place at which to
retire. There together with other old friends of the late king, they would have
recalled the inspiring days of Louis IX's rule and his companions' commitment
to the Capetian ruler's goals. Like so many aged men in similar situations, they
would have lamented the falling away from the old values that was already
a prominent theme in criticisms of the heir, Philip III (1270–85), and of his
court and his entourage.[12] Like elderly male friends nowadays, playing cards,
drinking beer and recalling the good old days, these churchmen, less the cards
and beer but perhaps with pear cider or apple compote in their stead, relived
in words the most rewarding time of their lives. This book tries to recover

---

7 Carolus-Barré, *Le procès de canonisation de saint Louis*, pp. 141–264; Jordan, *Men at the Center*, pp. 71–99.
8 Carolus-Barré, *Le procès de canonisation de saint Louis*, pp. 118–20; Jordan, *Tale of Two Monasteries*.
9 Fisquet, *France pontificale*, 8:30.
10 *Layettes*, 4:429–30 nos. 5662–3.
11 Masson-de-Saint-Amand, *Suite des essais historiques et anecdotiques*, p. 49.
12 Jordan, *Tale of Two Monasteries*, pp. 139–42.

something of the career and achievements of Philippe of Cahors, one of that imagined nostalgic company in Évreux, but one who neither wrote a book about the king nor lived long enough to offer his testimony to the papal commissioners at Saint-Denis on the man he most admired. Doing so, one hopes, will elucidate something more of the inner circle of Saint Louis's government, the nature of public service (the doing of good and, therefore, the bettering of the lot of common people, "le menu peuple") in the reformist state he engineered, and the linkage between service to the crown and service to God in the minds of thirteenth-century elites.

AN ECCLESIASTICAL CAREER TAKES SHAPE

In the preponderance of relevant Latin sources, the protagonist of this book appears as Philippus de Caturco (with minor spelling variations in the last element). Many books and articles render this as Philippe of Cahors, Cahors being the capital of the southwestern province of Quercy. This book adopts the same convention even though *de Caturco* can also be translated as "of Chaource," with reference to a completely different settlement, namely, either of two small villages in northeastern France.[13] It is unfortunate that the savants of the great early modern collection of sources on the medieval French church, the *Gallia christiana*, chose to favour with their considerable authority Chaource over Cahors. In a separate article, the reader will find a systematic review of all the relevant evidence on the matter, which provides an answer as to why they did so. A number of other inconsistencies and outright errors made since the seventeenth century in the establishment of a critical biography of Philippe of Cahors are also exposed in the article.[14]

The conclusions reached there may be stated briefly here. First, Philippe and a brother, named Pierre, came from a family passionately devoted to the Capetian rulers of France, one that supported the dynasty in its struggles with the Angevin kings of England. This in part explains the brothers' decision to seek employment – successfully – in French royal service. Such a pattern was not unusual for young men like these Cahorsins living in this period in the contested periphery of the medieval kingdom of France (meaning northern France). Around Louis IX, for example, these men included Geoffroy of Bar, dean of the cathedral chapter of Notre-Dame of Paris; Guillaume of Bray, a churchman expert in the canon law; Mathieu of Vendôme, councillor in

---

13 Jordan, "Philippe of Cahors; Or, What's in a Name?"
14 Jordan, "Philippe of Cahors; Or, What's in a Name?"

Parlement and abbot of Saint-Denis; Robert of Douai, royal physician; and Robert of Sorbon, university professor, court chaplain and preacher, cathedral canon, and founder of the Sorbonne.[15]

The evidence is conclusive that Philippe of Cahors's lineage was solidly bourgeois. Other burgher members of his extended family were also fiercely loyal to the French crown. This devotion manifested itself both in helping bankroll the conquests of Simon I de Montfort (d. 1218) during the Albigensian Crusade and in facilitating in the mid-thirteenth century the extension of French influence in Languedoc, where the extended family came to acquire significant properties in and near Pézenas. Several members of the lineage appear to have been rewarded for their support. In two cases they received appointments to canonries in Parisian foundations, one at the collegial church of Saint-Médard and the other at the cathedral of Notre-Dame.[16]

Traditional native Parisian elites in general probably looked askance at Cahorsins as geographical and linguistic marginals (they were notorious for their bad and badly accented Latin and French). Moreover, northerners would have expected men of Cahors to be stained by the moral taint of usury, the latter's practise of which was also notorious. The very word "Cahorsin" was a synonym for usurer.[17] Louis IX may in general have shared these prejudices, but not every Cahorsin succumbed to the same moral faults. Those who rose above the expectations of their backgrounds and adhered to an exemplary morality found a patron in the king. He may even have relished opportunities to support them, because of the devotion his generosity engendered in them towards him as their patron.[18]

Documentary evidence establishes that Philippe of Cahors's career was in full swing by 1252. Knowing this and given the position he held at the time (see below), he would then have been a man in his early or mid-thirties. How did he enter into service? A family of burgher standing with aspirations for its offspring to serve in an ecclesiastical or any of the many secular administrations – municipal, aristocratic, or royal – needed to invest some of its resources in educating its male children in reading Latin and learning to do at least simple arithmetic (literacy and numeracy). Tutoring was available from local priests, but scholars have also discovered that parish and, in some towns, municipally operated grammar schools teaching reading and the abacus were much more

---

15 Jordan, *Tale of Two Monasteries*, p. 25; Jordan, *Men at the Center*, pp. 3, 17–18, 20.
16 The documentation and argument may be found in Jordan, "Philippe of Cahors; Or, What's in a Name?"
17 Grunwald, "Lombards, Cahorsins and Jews," pp. 393–4.
18 This argument is advanced in Jordan, *Men at the Center*, pp. 16–22.

extensive in Europe in the High Middle Ages than was once thought to be the case.[19] Cahors, counting its cathedral, had eleven medieval parishes,[20] and thus in all likelihood eleven *écoles paroissiales*.

From parish and municipal schools able boys could advance to the cathedral schools. Cahors's cathedral school had a distinguished pedigree by the thirteenth century, having flourished since the Carolingian era.[21] It enjoyed modest fame for its introductory training in civil and canon law.[22] Evidence from as early as the eleventh century shows that its attendees included a number of young men who went on to become capable writers and scholars in many fields, penning works as disparate as Latin chronicles and vernacular troubadour poetry.[23] At some point Philippe decided to take clerical orders, but he also opted to continue his studies in law.

He did so almost certainly at the University of Orléans, where he would have been a member of the Aquitanian nation or division.[24] The survival rate of records from French provincial universities in the first century of their existence tends to be low. That for Orléans is a little better than most,[25] but it is not great. Nonetheless, a considerable amount of information concerning its academic culture survives. For several reasons the university drew adolescents and young men to it from a wide geographical area, reflected in the designation of the nations or the divisions of the school: "Francia, Lotharingia, Alemannia, Burgundia, Campania, Normannia, Picardia, Turonia, Scocia, Aquitania."[26] Most universities had fewer nations, often just four. This does not necessarily signify that there was less regional diversity in their student bodies, a fact that has to be determined from other sources.[27] The larger number of nations at Orléans may be an indication of a particularly high degree of geographical and ethnic diversity.

---

19 Verger, *Culture, enseignement et société*, pp. 25–41. See also Willemsen, *Back to the Schoolyard*, pp. 29–30.
20 Marquette, "Pouvoir ecclésiastique et espace urbain," p. 26; *Pouillé du diocèse de Cahors*, nos. 124, 138–45.
21 *Dictionnaire de pédagogie*, part 1, II, 1711.
22 *Dictionnaire de pédagogie*, part 1, II, 1711.
23 *Dictionnaire de pédagogie*, part 1, II, 1711.
24 Grandmottet, "Officialités de Reims," pp. 80, 103; cf. Forcadet, "Les premiers juges de la Cour du roi," p. 254.
25 Jullien de Pommerol and Monfrin, "Archives des universités médiévales," pp. 8–10.
26 Jullien de Pommerol and Monfrin, "Archives des universités médiévales," p. 11; Rashdall, *Universities of Europe in the Middle Ages*, 2:146, 150.
27 Kibre, *Nations in the Medieval Universities*, p. 18, Rashdall, *Universities of Europe in the Middle Ages*, vol. 3, index, p. 536, s.v. "Nations."

What explains or helps to explain this diversity at a provincial university? While the University of Paris was a far more prestigious institution than the University of Orléans, civil law was not part of the curriculum in the capital at the time Philippe undertook professional study. Indeed, many scholars believe it was the migration of Parisian masters to Orléans after Pope Honorius III's prohibition in 1219 of teaching Roman law at Paris that provided the initial opportunity for the schools of the provincial city to transform themselves into a university.[28] Honorius's prohibition was instrumental in Orléans's success, since the school would become famous for legal education.[29] The subsequent diaspora or Great Dispersion of scholars and students, many of whom came to Orléans, during the suspension of most academic lectures in Paris during a long strike over student immunities in 1229[30] was the event that sealed the transformation of the nascent provincial university into a major institution of higher education.

Students at the law school in Orléans and at law schools in general in the period tended to come from financially secure and upwardly striving bourgeois families.[31] Having legal training was useful for men like Philippe, men about to embark on administrative careers.[32] Coming from an administrative family, as I have argued Philippe did, he would have found his time at the law school of Orléans in the 1240s a valuable stepping stone in general. It was one of noticeable value for a young man hoping someday to enter service, perhaps even, like his brother Pierre, *royal* service in the north or in Paris in particular. Indeed, by the mid-thirteenth century, formal legal training, largely at Orléans, was almost de rigueur for the educational résumé of middling and higher-level administrators, including those sitting as advisers around the king or in the High Court, the institution later known as *Parlement*.[33] Those who yearned for administrative positions elsewhere, say, in Languedoc, might have preferred other universities, like the University of Toulouse or the University of Montpellier, where a man could come to a local prelate's or aristocrat's notice or to that of the king's provincial representatives.[34]

---

28 Jullien de Pommerol and Monfrin, "Archives des universités médiévales," p. 7.
29 Jullien de Pommerol and Monfrin, "Archives des universités médiévales," p. 7; Berthe, "Élites urbaines," p. 32.
30 Young, *Scholarly Community at the Early University of Paris*, pp. 81–3.
31 Jullien de Pommerol and Monfrin, "Archives des universités médiévales," p. 17.
32 Jullien de Pommerol and Monfrin, "Archives des universités médiévales," p. 17.
33 Menes, "Premiers acteurs de la vie parlementaire," p. 165.
34 Cf. Jullien de Pommerol and Monfrin, "Archives des universités médiévales," p. 8; Berthe, "Élites urbaines," p. 32.

Philippe's model, if he needed or had one, may have been the idealized career of one of the most famous holy men whom the region of his origin produced, Saint Didier (Desiderius). Didier, from Albi by birth, fifty miles (approximately eighty kilometres) southwest of Cahors, lived in Merovingian times, according to his *vita*.[35] At his mother's urging, the narrative explained, he lived an ascetic life. He also received an excellent education that included the study of Roman law. For most of his career, he served the Merovingian kings, rising to high administrative office before becoming the bishop of Cahors. Half a millennium after Didier's death, people familiar with his legend well knew that training in law remained a useful entry into royal service.

Philippe of Cahors's career did not commence in royal service, however. He was earlier employed as *officialis* of the court of the archdeacon of the archdiocese of Reims, from June of 1252 until 31 August 1256.[36] *Officiales* were men with substantial legal knowledge. They drafted documents and participated in judicial cases involving the rights of the prelates and the ecclesiastical corporations they served.[37] An act of 7 January 1256 (new style) provides Philippe's full title, "Magister Philippus de Caturco, officialis curie domini Octoboni, Sancti Adriani diaconi cardinalis, Remensis archidiaconi."[38] The title *magister* implies that Philippe had been well educated. More important for his standing in the ecclesiastical community of the time and in his relations with secular authorities was the fact that he was the *officialis* of the judicial court of an influential man, Ottobuono Fieschi.

It was not the archidiaconate of Reims per se that endowed Ottobuono with influence. He was an unusual prelate. Besides being a canon of the cathedral chapter of Reims and, indeed, the chapter's chancellor in the middle and late 1240s down to 1250, he was elevated the next year to the cardinalate, assuming the title of cardinal deacon of Saint-Adrian. In the same period, indeed for a quarter of a century (ca. 1245–70), this pluralist also held a canonry in the cathedral chapter of Notre-Dame of Paris. Ottobuono travelled much in all these years, including those of his archidiaconate in Reims.[39] While he was away, he entrusted to Philippe of Cahors, as long as the latter served as the

---

35 Mathisen, "Desiderius of Cahors," pp. 455–69.
36 Grandmottet, "Officialités de Reims," pp. 86, 103.
37 Fournier, *Les officialités au moyen âge.*
38 Delisle, "Chronologie des baillis et des sénéchaux royaux," p. 26* n. 19, citing the first cartulary of Saint-Médard de Soissons; Laon, Archives Départementales de l'Aisne, folio 13 v. 1 confirmed Delisle's citation; http://regecart.irht.cnrs.fr/dossier-715-TO1/ms-0578 and http://regecart.irht.cnrs.fr/dossier-713-R1/ms-0578.
39 Schöpp, *Papst Hadrian V*, pp. 35–71.

officialis of his court, all the duties he could. In other words, Philippe was by default the active centre of judicial administration in the archdeaconry in the early 1250s, interacting as the archdeacon himself would otherwise have had to interact if he had not travelled so often. On 16 January 1254, Pope Innocent IV issued a long and detailed formal delineation of the various powers of the archbishop of Reims and the archdeacon.[40] By good fortune, in the same document the pontiff also solemnized the relationship just described between the archdeacon and his *officialis,* Philippe of Cahors.[41] Philippe's handling of his duties, such as interacting with litigants of various social classes, brought him considerable notice in the city and cathedral, both of which, as the coronation site, were enormously significant in French royal self-perception.

Philippe's work as *officialis* was as varied as the matters affecting the archdeaconry of Reims itself. Sometimes it was routine, as one would expect. For example, Philippe exercised the archdeacon's gracious jurisdiction, which is to say, he offered his court as a registry of concords on the conveyancing of property involving people or institutions living within the archdeaconry's ban. These concords then had formal records maintained in the archdeacon's judicial archives that the parties could consult if disputes later arose. The preparation of the documents and their recognition in the archdeacon's court in the presence of the parties and others affected by the transactions provided the *officialis* with the opportunity to meet and interact with local landholders, including prominent laypeople. Such was the case in a purchase of a vineyard in this grape-growing area of the archdiocese in April 1253. The purchaser was the abbey of Saint-Nicaise. The sellers were eight individuals, including a number of women: Supplicie, the widow of Jean Dagay of the village of Fusy; a certain Roger and his wife Gertrude; Oidelète and Luquète (Supplicie's daughters); Evrard (Luquète's husband); Garnier (Supplicie's son); and the widow Hélisende of Fusy. Philippe used the local priest of the village of Sermiers (*département* of the Marne) as his intermediary in arranging for the public declaration of the sale in the immediate vicinity of the property (*in territorio de Sarmiers*). The priest or his agent delivered the final documents to the *officialis* in Reims. He reviewed, sealed, and published them in open air on 27 April.[42]

A man in Philippe's position also had to arbitrate, at best, or when arbitration failed, adjudicate among various churchmen in disputes over their rights or the extent of their jurisdiction. In the adjudication of one such dispute at

40 *Archives administratives de Reims*, 1, part 2, pp. 746–56.
41 *Archives administratives de Reims*, 1, part 2, pp. 750–1, 754.
42 *Chartular von Saint-Nicaise in Reims*, pp. 183–5 nos. 74–5.

which Philippe presided in January 1256 (new style) the issue was the division of the rights, and therefore the division of the revenues, that each of two local priests had in a chapel dedicated to Saint Memmius.[43] Memmius was reputed to have been the first bishop of Châlons-sur-Marne, the present-day Châlons-en-Champagne in the *département* of the Marne. Like so many early bishops in Gaul, he was credited with large-scale conversions of the local pagan population, hence his sanctity; and his reputation was enhanced by the holiness of other family members, in his case that of his sister Saint Poma, virgin. His cult was not widespread. Cult centres, judging from French village names (Menge, Memmie), were scarce beyond the Châlonnais. But the saint's interventions and miraculous healings had been reported at least since the sixth century.[44] Pilgrims' oblations probably enhanced the revenues of the chapel of Saint-Memmius, the focal point of the dispute. A tedious review of the evidence in order to resolve the dispute was part of the judicial *officialis*'s job.

A perhaps more revealing indicator of Philippe's character emerges from another case, one that saw him issue a definitive judgment in a binding arbitration of a dispute between churchmen, on the one hand, and a yeoman farmer and his servants, on the other.[45] This rustic, Garnier the Cheerful or the Wanton (*Warner le Gode* in the Latin document), appears to have been a proprietor of some wealth. He violated the rights of the abbey of Saint-Thiérry by using its lands for the illicit passage of his livestock – sheep, goats, cattle, and swine. He had his men provide them with fodder seized from the abbey's fields. He also had them transport goods in part of a waterway over which the monks claimed lordship. The latter were distressed that Garnier offered only ten pounds recompense when they first raised the issue of his despicable actions (*dedecus*). The monks regarded his behaviour as a more serious breach than he did, in part because he made counterclaims, alleging that they had exaggerated the territorial extent of the abbey's property. They must have impugned Garnier for other acts as well, charges that were less well founded and that he contested. A non-specific reference to these other charges and their denial (*per assertionem et negationem partium*), and his absolution (*absolvo ab impetitione abbatis et conventus*) with regard to them made it into the definitive judgment.

In his role as *officialis* Philippe handed down this judgment on 27 June 1254. He appears to have reserved the matter of damages (*expensarum questione reservata*), from which one can probably infer that he was going to affirm the

---

43 Referenced from the first cartulary of Saint-Médard of Soissons; http://regecart.irht.cnrs.fr/dossier-713-R1/ms-0578.

44 Cooke, "Menges," p. 436.

45 *Archives administratives de Reims*, 1, part 2, pp. 759–61.

ten-pound sum. With the full panoply of judicial experts and others who sat on the archdeacon's court, at which he presided, however, the *officialis* rejected Garnier's challenge to the territorial extent of the abbey of Saint-Thiérry's holdings. The language was resolute. Not only did the judgment affirm the boundaries, as described by the monks, it warned Garnier not to drive his livestock through the lands defined by these extensive boundaries. He could not pasture any of his livestock on those lands, and he could not use any of the watercourses that belonged to the abbey without the monks' express permission. To put it another way, payment of ten pounds or for that matter of any sum of money was no licence to renew trampling on the monks' rights. What role his councillors (*bonorum virorum et jurisperitorum communicato consilio*) played in the *officialis* reaching this decision is unknown, but if the decision implies an emphatic distaste for wantonly abusive laypeople, one can interpret it as aligning Philippe's temperament with that of the king he would later serve. However, it is only fair to add that at least one early historian has, without further explanation, cast the dispute as one of peasant resentment at churchmen's purchases of properties once considered "common," in which case what Garnier had cheerfully done was an assertion of traditional rights, not a transgression at all.[46]

In any case, it was working for Archdeacon Ottobuono that provided the kinds of experiences and on-the-job training in a legal venue for Philippe. The archdeacon's career has additional relevance for Philippe's story. Ottobuono was on the rise. Dante would later stigmatize this fellow Italian as avaricious because of his evident careerism and then consign him to purgatory in the *Commedia*.[47] Whatever the churchman's true character (and Dante was not a disinterested witness), Ottobuono did become an increasingly significant presence in high ecclesiastical and international politics. In the mid-1260s, the member of Louis IX's inner circle, Gui Foucois, who became Pope Clement IV made Ottobuono a papal legate to England; hence the scholarly notice of his career in the *Oxford Dictionary of National Biography*. There he became involved in the diplomatic morass that surrounded King Henry III, his magnates, and his brother-in-law, King Louis IX, and their attempts to resolve the English Barons' War.[48]

Ottobuono's position as legate, like his earlier positions in the 1240s and 1250s that also precipitated near constant interaction with high-profile English

---

46 Rivière, *Histoire des biens communaux*, pp. 314–15.
47 Dante, *Purgatorio*, canto 19, lines 88–145 (Hollander translation).
48 Bolton, "Ottobuono," *Oxford Dictionary of National Biography*, http://www.oxforddnb.com /view/article/50348.

and French secular leaders, furnished him with opportunities to bring the names of bright and assiduous young men, men like Philippe of Cahors, to the attention of those who could utilize them in their administrations. His familial relations made for another significant platform for securing privileged access to and perhaps the trust of members of the English and French elite. Otto-buono's sister was married to Count Thomas II of Savoy, who was a kinsman of the four Provençal *dominae* who married King Henry III of England and his brother, Earl Richard of Cornwall, and King Louis IX of France and his brother, Count Charles of Anjou. The culminating glory of Ottobuono Fieschi's career, his elevation as Pope Adrian V in 1276, was short-lived, "one month and a little more" (*Un mese e poco più*), in Dante's words.[49] Yet, if I am correct, his career as a whole had enormous ramifications for those who worked with him and earned his respect.

I would conclude that sometime during his time as archdeacon, Ottobuono recommended his *officialis* to an administrator or administrators who had the power to secure the able Cahorsin a place in royal government. Who might these have been? The royal administrative presence in the area around Reims was felt through the crown's *baillis* or chief regional governors in Vermandois and Senlis, two *bailliages* that were sometimes managed jointly.[50] The *baillis* and many other high-ranking members of the "French field administration" made official trips, in the case of Vermandois/Senlis three times a year, to Paris to have their accounts audited and to pursue whatever judicial or disciplinary business they had in the king's High Court.[51] In the period during which Philippe was Archdeacon Ottobuono's *officialis*, one *bailli* of Vermandois seems a likely conduit for information on our man to reach the royal court. This is Pierre of Fontaines, who studied at the law school in Orléans and went on to have a long and distinguished career in *Parlement*.[52] He is also renowned as the author of the *Conseil*, one of the most important legal treatises of the thirteenth century, a book that a recent scholar has argued ought also to be understood as an instructional text for the elder sons in Louis IX's household.[53]

---

49 Dante, *Purgatorio*, canto 19, line 103 (Mandelbaum translation; see the note for an unconvincing alternative identification).

50 Jordan, *Louis IX and the Challenge of the Crusade*, pp. 47, 226–7.

51 Fesler, "French Field Administration," pp. 76–111.

52 Griffiths, "Les Origines et la carrière de Pierre de Fontaines," pp. 544–67; Griffiths, "*New Men among the Lay Counselors* of Saint Louis' *Parlement*," pp. 233, 241, 243–4, 247–51, 254, 257, 260, 267; Forcadet, "Les premiers juges de la Cour du roi," pp. 256–7.

53 For the book, see Pierre de Fontaines, *Le Conseil*. For its purpose (in part) as a textbook of moral righteousness in the operation of the law, see Föller, *Königskinder: Erziehung am Hof Ludwigs IX*, pp. 67–81.

In whatever way Philippe's reputation became more widely known – by Ottobuono's dissemination, through a communication from Pierre of Fontaines, or otherwise – what is certain is that Philippe changed jobs in 1257. He left his position as *officialis* of the archdeacon's court at Reims on 31 August 1256 and departed for Paris soon after, where a few months later he began to serve in the king's High Court. Here was proof of the observation of one French scholar of how easily churchmen involved in doing ecclesiastical justice could move into secular administration ("officiaux et archidiacres, grâce aux études qu'ils ont faites, peuvent aussi accéder aux charges importantes de la vie civile").[54]

---

54 Grandmottet, "Officialités de Reims," p. 81.

2

A SWIFT ASCENT: FROM JUNIOR CLERK TO "CHANCELLOR"

Philippe of Cahors may have visited Paris on business on any number of occasions before he took up residence in the late summer of 1256. Yet, being in the city on business was not the same as full-time employment there. One did not just walk into the chambers of the *Parlement* of Paris and set to work. There was a steep learning curve. It was *sine qua non* that one present oneself as a well-educated and experienced man. We have no evidence of tests, as the guild masters in Paris sometimes administered, to determine minimal competence in a craft before admission as an apprentice.[1] Was there a preliminary determination as to whether a would-be clerk of *Parlement* had sufficient reading and writing knowledge of Latin or other expertise, as contemporary churchmen took?[2] Probably so, but the recommendations of noteworthy referees, like Archdeacon Ottobuono, might obviate a language exam and otherwise lessen the interrogation in the first interview. Nevertheless, the officers of the court would have compelled new men to pledge solemnly to carry out their work honestly and competently and indeed swear to do so on the gospels or on relics, as some guilds required their officials to do.[3]

Newly hired clerks, even those with legal training, needed to acquire familiarity with the particulars of the High Court's jurisdiction, and they needed to do so expeditiously. They needed to know what coercive powers belonged to them to gather information for the judges and councillors. Caution dictated that they also find out what sanctions they would face if they exceeded the limits of the powers they wielded. As rapidly as possible, new appointees to the clerical staff also had to achieve something like instant recall of the judicial procedures

---

1 Farmer, *Silk Industries of Medieval Paris*, p. 115.
2 *Register of Eudes of Rouen*, pp. 174, 191–2, 237–8, 379–80, 450–1.
3 Farmer, *Silk Industries of Medieval Paris*, p. 121.

followed for trials and arbitrations and of the proper wording of oaths. At least partial mastery of the substantive law applicable in various sorts of cases, including precedents specific to the High Court, was another desideratum. Finally, there were distinctive documentary conventions – script, verbal formulas, and sealing practices, among others – that the clerks needed to employ and had to, with dispatch, commit to memory. Not all of this acquisition of knowledge was or could be preliminary. There must have been a great deal of learning on the job, through observation of and listening to cases argued by experienced judges (masters), lawyers, and senior clerks.

Besides the specialized tutelage into the formal work of the institution, newcomers required initiation into professional protocols. *Parlement* was no ordinary judicial forum. The king himself was present at many sessions, as were, regularly, bishops and abbots, nobles and senior judges. What gestures were required to greet and express due respect when these men entered and left the chamber? During the sessions, how were the clerks to address them? When and where could one sit in their presence? What prayers did men pray to open and to close the sessions? What hymns did they sing? Under what circumstances was it appropriate to interrupt the great men when they spoke, and if one did need to interrupt, what formulaic apologies should one employ? In particular, did the protocols oblige neophytes to remain silent until called upon? What kind of admonitions followed any of the several possible breaches of etiquette, who issued rebukes, and how many demerits, so to speak, could appear on one's record before reprimands gave way to punishments, perhaps even dismissal? How many clerks failed to rise to the necessary level of competence with sufficient celerity and faced termination? Finally, what length of time was typical before a circumspect and hard-working clerk escaped the intense scrutiny that fell on all newcomers, and became a genuine colleague in this august body? Such questions confronted Philippe of Cahors on the first and many subsequent days, weeks, and months after the offer and his acceptance of a job on the court's staff.

Philippe's last recorded piece of business done as curial *officialis* of the archdeacon of Reims took place on 31 August 1256. The adjustment to and command of the various procedures and protocols of his new job at the *Parlement* were sufficiently advanced a year later that he could play a useful role in a case resolved in September 1257. Before we turn to the substance of this case, however, there is one additional preliminary point to make. The royal fiscal accounts of the mid-century are replete with references to allocations for robes for many of the crown's officials.[4] However, clerks needed a great deal

---

4 *Recueil des historiens des Gaules et de la France* (hereafter cited as *HF*), 21:274, 279, 281, 289, etc.

more than an occasional robe to subsist on, and Paris was an expensive city. They had to pay for their lodging, clothing (less the robes), food and drink, and non-business travel, trips that their royal employer did not reimburse or pay for directly. It is possible that these clerks were pious men, indeed, that their piety as much as their intelligence and work experience helped to bring them to the king's attention. Piety could be costly for those whose faith prompted them to give gifts to the church or alms directly to the poor. Other pastimes, also costly, would not have pleased the king and were ruinous, if discovered, to career advancement, as his numerous dismissals in other contexts made manifest.[5] Paris offered louche pleasures aplenty in the thirteenth and fourteenth century: gambling haunts, taverns in great numbers, and prostitutes, even though Louis IX strove diligently to eradicate the "vices" that he reviled as polluting his city.[6] Those clerks who were nevertheless drawn to the vices and unable or unwilling to resist needed to be hyper-cautious, and they needed money to indulge themselves. Where did it come from, this money, whatever use, uplifting or degrading, they chose to put it to?

The churchmen serving in *Parlement* most often lived off the income of ecclesiastical offices, benefices and prebends (the terminology varies) in the king's gift, and were wholly or almost wholly non-residents of those offices.[7] The system, employed not solely by kings but also by dukes and counts, was a complex one and not easy to understand in its entirety at this distance in time.[8] Nonetheless, at its simplest it depended on a delegation of authority from the prebendary to a resident cleric who, for a modest share of the revenues that endowed the office, did the work, much as Philippe of Cahors had performed the judicial work in Reims for his often-absent archdeacon. In the first appearance of Philippe by name in the *Olim*, the records of *Parlement*, the scribe responsible identified him as a *magister* and *clericus Regis*. The record also notes his possession of the prebend of treasurer (*thesaurarius*) of the cathedral church of Bayeux in Normandy.[9] There is no evidence that in all his years in

---

5 Joinville, *Vie de saint Louis*, pp. 246–9, paras. 170–1.

6 For proscriptions of gaming in various texts, see Richard, *Saint Louis*, p. 282, and Le Goff, *Saint Louis*, p. 218, and for evidence of gambling dens, see *Confessions et jugements de criminels*, pp. 185–6. On taverns and prostitution and attempts to regulate the first and hyper-regulate the second, see Baldwin, *Masters, Princes and Merchants*, 1:133–7; Châtelain, "Notes sur quelques tavernes," pp. 87–109; Nowacka, "Persecution, Marginalization, or Tolerance," pp. 175–96.

7 Griffiths, "St. Louis and the New Clerks of *Parlement*," pp. 269–76; Griffiths, "Capetian Kings and St. Martin of Tours," pp. 85, 103.

8 Massoni, "Les collégiales royales, ducales et comtales," pp. 37–9; Montaubin, "Raoul Grosparmi," pp. 428–9.

9 *Olim*, 1:20 no. xv; Grandmottet, "Officialités de Reims," pp. 81, 103.

Paris Philippe's relationship with the see of Bayeux was anything other than nominal and financial.

In time – that is, as he assumed more responsibility and his duties increased in Paris – Philippe received additional benefices that were in the king's gift. He became a pluralist. The system from which he was profiting could have led to weakness in the home churches from which the revenues for his income came, but under Louis IX the government made strenuous efforts, successful or not, to ensure that worthy men were carrying out the duties.[10] Our clerk would later also collect the revenues (or a substantial part thereof) of the office of *scholasticus*, director of education, of the cathedral school of Bayeux, according to a document dated 18 December 1262.[11] Around the same time, in 1261/62 he was made treasurer of Saint-Hilary of Poitiers.[12] Still later, he assumed the office of treasurer of the collegiate church of Saint-Frambourg (or, as it is sometimes rendered, Frambours or Frambaud) of Senlis,[13] before his election as bishop of Évreux in 1269, at which time he resigned the benefices he was holding.

Churchmen had no monopoly on honesty, but what the combined income from possessing multiple benefices assured those who ascended to high levels in royal government was that they had no obvious *need*, even in a city with as many attractive and expensive luxuries as Paris, to take money under the table. For the same reason the French kings paid enormous salaries to the *baillis* and *sénéchaux* who served them as regional governors, twenty or so men at any one time in the reign of Louis IX.[14] The sentiment endured for centuries. Affluent and propertied men were the preferred appointees to high administrative and advisory posts in early liberal states, like nineteenth-century Britain, because the crown perceived them, rightly or wrongly, to be immune or almost immune from the seduction of bribery.[15] It did not make them immune from

---

10 William of Chartres, "On the Life and Deeds of Louis," in *Sanctity of Louis IX*, pp. 93–4, para. 20; Joinville, *Vie de saint Louis*, p. 562, para. 692; Griffiths, "Capetian Kings and St. Martin of Tours," p. 103.

11 *Archives administratives de Reims*, 1, part 2, p. 844. See also Grandmottet, "Officialités de Reims," p. 103; Fisquet, *France pontificale*, 8:29; Chassant and Sauvage, *Histoire des évêques d'Évreux*, p. 75.

12 Perrichet, *Grande chancellerie*, p. 171.

13 Fisquet, *France pontificale*, 8:29; Perrichet, *Grande chancellerie*, p. 196; Chassant and Sauvage, *Histoire des évêques d'Évreux*, p. 75; Grandmottet, "Officialités de Reims," p. 103.

14 Richard, "Les Conseillers de saint Louis," p. 141; Carolus-Barré, "Les Baillis de Philippe le Hardi," p. 132.

15 Gash, *Aristocracy and People*; Campbell, *The Civil Service in Britain*; Prochaska, *Women and Philanthropy in Nineteenth-Century England*. Whether the erosion of independent fortune has contributed to the present increase in government corruption in Britain (alleged in O'Toole, *Ideal of Public Service*, pp. 5, 10, 15) is an open question.

other temptations, not least arrogance, imperiousness, and self-righteousness, as Trollope satirized.[16] However that may be, pluralism per se, although often decried by critics of the medieval church and typed by historians as one form of corruption, could actually help prevent other forms.

CAREER IN *PARLEMENT*

The cases in *Parlement* in which Philippe of Cahors participated give some impression of the issues and sorts of people a professionally trained *clerc du roi* had to reckon with. On a loose leaf of parchment inserted between folios twelve and thirteen of the *Olim*, one finds a memorandum that relates to a case from 1257 summarily reported in the codex itself and is the first to name Philippe as a participant.[17] The case in the summary enrolment, which does not name him (he had not yet achieved prominence in the court), is the digest of an inquest into a claim made by the crown that jurisdiction over counterfeiters, meaning people who actually counterfeited and/or used counterfeit coins knowingly, pertained to the king in the village of Villeneuve-Saint-Georges, just southeast of Paris. This claim rested on a larger one that the crown asserted to the possession of high or capital justice over malefactors arrested in the village or on the highway (*via publica*) that ran through Villeneuve. The abbot of Saint-Germain-des-Prés of Paris disputed these assertions, responding that counterfeiters apprehended in the village fell under his jurisdiction. The inquest (as noted, the names of those who carried it out are *not* provided in the enrolled record) decided that the superior claim to jurisdiction over counterfeiters lay with the abbot, but the larger issue of high justice was reserved. In other words, *Parlement* was unwilling at this point on the basis of available evidence to say that the abbot's jurisdiction over counterfeiters was anything more than an eccentric sort of privilege, leaving high justice in principle in the crown's possession (*non racione alte justicie, quia non est determinatum utrum sit alta justicia aut non*). The crown's procurators also had evidence of the king earlier exercising capital justice with respect to rape/abduction (*de raptu*) in Villeneuve. The implication was that if jurisdiction *de raptu* was in the crown's possession, other pleas of high justice were, unless there was specific evidence to the contrary.

So much for the formal case record. The loose parchment memorandum inserted into the *Olim* provides the background for this inquest and decision,

---

16 Halperin, "Fiction That Is True," pp. 179–95; Sullivan, *Literature in the Public Service*, pp. 65–113; Taylor, *Hostility to Aristocracy in Late Nineteenth- and Early Twentieth-Century Britain.*

17 *Olim*, 1:19–20 no. xv (and no. 1).

specifying also the two men, including Philippe of Cahors, appointed to investigate the matter, information absent from the formal record. This investigation is revealing of the unpleasant situation on the ground in and about Villeneuve-Saint-Georges that provoked it. The story began in May 1257 with the arrest of two counterfeiters in the village, one while fleeing through the nearby fields onto the highway, the other while still in the marketplace. Following their apprehension and the guilty verdict at their trial, the court handed the malefactors over to two knights in the service of the abbot of Saint-Germain who saw to their execution by hanging from the monastery's gallows in the village. The *prévôts* of Paris, the crown's chief administrative and police officials of the city and its banlieu at the time, protested that the abbot had infringed on the king's jurisdiction. Before making a final decision as to who was correct, the king, on the advice of legal experts, ordered that the malefactors' corpses be taken down from the monastery's gallows and, pending further inquiry, rehanged from gallows erected on land held in common by the abbot and himself. As long as the resolution of the dispute was still up in the air, the corpses would also be.

Parlement assigned Philippe of Cahors and a lay associate, a knight named Jean, presumably another junior clerk, to the investigation. One can imagine the searching of record evidence and the taking of depositions, all unmentioned but comparable to the process in other cases. Master Philippe and *le chevalier* Jean presented their findings to *Parlement* when it assembled in Melun in September. Besides Philippe, an array of royal clerks, lay and ecclesiastical, was present at the session. Based on Philippe and Jean's investigation, the court found in favour of the abbey of Saint-Germain, represented that day by its procurator. The judgment affirmed the abbot's claim to counterfeiters caught either in Villeneuve-Saint-Georges *or* on the king's highway in its territory, for in the grisly scene in the environs of Villeneuve that played out following the court's decision it was the corpses of both malefactors, though captured in quite different venues, that labourers again took down. The labourers then dismantled the temporary gallows from which the counterfeiters had been hanging across the river from the village on land held in common by the king and the abbot and cast the structure into the water (*dicte furce communes ... fuerunt destructe et projecte in aqua*). They transported the malefactors' cadavers back to the original gallows belonging to the abbey in Villeneuve and rehanged them there in a public display (*dicti suspensi asportati et resuspensi coram populo ad primas furcas*), dramatically signifying the vindication of the abbot's claim. Nevertheless, the last clause of the record, *et viature justicia liberata*, meaning that "*viatura* jurisdiction was handed over" to the abbot, finessed the argument over high justice, which was not implied by the word *viatura*.

This investigation was the sort of work junior clerks would carry out. It was not necessarily pleasant business. The reading of documents, which do not appear to have been dispositive one way or the other on the nature of the abbey's and the crown's jurisdiction, required supplementary on-site inquiry in order to determine precisely where the authorities apprehended the criminals and whether the locations fell under the abbatial or royal ban. It might have been possible to avoid the sight of the bodies hanging from the gallows, although part of the ritual – the rehanging on neutral territory as a sign of the contested jurisdiction – was in fact intended as a very public display, whose sight was hard to avoid. The investigation took place during the summer and was not resolved until September, during which time the bodies rotted and the stench was manifest at every puff of wind. It would have been worse to be the menial labourers who had to hang and then unhang and rehang and then again unhang and rehang the bodies. Most of this foulness the clerks could have managed to avoid. The real advantage for junior men like Philippe was that they made contacts with people of substance in carrying out an investigation. These would have included knights in service to the abbey of Saint-Germain des Prés, the abbot of such a great monastery himself or at least his procurator, and the *prévôts* of Paris, all influential men with whom the clerks could expect to interact repeatedly in the course of their careers. This mirrored Philippe's experience in Reims, but now his circle of contacts widened because of the expansive reach of the court he served.

Philippe's role in *Parlement* became more prominent over time, and he participated in resolving higher-profile conflicts. In one of these, his earlier experience in Reims served him particularly well. From at least 1259 deep into the 1260s and even later, the crown was involved in a three-way dispute with the archbishop of Reims and the monastery of Saint-Remi of Reims over the possession of the guard of the monastery.[18] Frederic Cheyette has treated the issue of the royal safeguard in France, its roots in the Merovingian period, and its development down through the fourteenth century.[19] Broadly speaking those communities, either ecclesiastical or lay, that fell under someone's safeguard were supposed to be able to call upon that someone for help when they felt that their rights and privileges were under threat of encroachment or illegal seizure.

In some instances, this recourse was a mixed blessing. The furthest extension of the concept of safeguard was the system of temporal regalia that vested in the crown the right to collect the revenues of dioceses or abbeys when their

---

18 Tillemont, *Vie de saint Louis*, 4:197–9.
19 Cheyette, "Royal Safeguard in Medieval France," pp. 631–52.

headship was vacant and therefore when they most likely would benefit from powerful outsiders' protection.[20] Then again, sometimes they needed protection from their protectors. Less scrupulous kings than Louis IX appropriated vast sums by way of temporal regalia, and managed sometimes, by the use of technicalities, to extend the vacancies in order to increase their take.[21] Safeguard in general, even when it was of a lesser sort than that implied by the right to temporal regalia and whether vested in a king or another potentate, always came at a price – financial *and* psychological, as it subjected otherwise semi-autonomous communities to intense external oversight and downright interference.

The attention that Cheyette paid to the law of safeguard, to claims and counterclaims to the right over specific communities, and the consequences of its exercise in Louis IX's reign per se is thin. He excused the thinness of his treatment by referencing the absence of a comprehensive list of royal *acta* for the king's reign, a fact, he asserted, that made conclusions drawn from research on safeguard in the period inconclusive at best.[22] Although the long-planned comprehensive calendar of the king's *acta* is still not available,[23] there is plenty of evidence on how safeguard spread, how it worked, and how zealously lords defended their right to exercise it both against counterclaimants and over the communities on whose behalf they exercised it. The king's dispute with the archbishop of Reims, Thomas of Beaumes, which came to a head in 1259, throws light on some of the salient issues in the years Louis ruled, what Cheyette overdramatically referred to as a "dark age" for exploring the history of safeguard.[24]

Thomas of Beaumes was archbishop of Reims from 1251 to 1263, during the entire time Philippe of Cahors was Archdeacon Ottobuono's *officalis* there. The experience gave Philippe the kind of feel for local conditions and rivalries that could provide valuable insight into and guidance for a dispute of this sort. The case had been meandering through *Parlement*, with the various sides disputing the claims of the others for a long time; the records read as if there was ever-mounting exasperation.[25] The king in particular was weary of the con-

---

20 Campbell, "Temporal and Spiritual Regalia," pp. 351–83.

21 Jordan, *Louis IX and the Challenge of the Crusade*, pp. 150 and 150–1 no. 97.

22 Cheyette, "Royal Safeguard in Medieval France," p. 640.

23 Session, 27 June 1980, *Académie des Inscriptions et Belles Lettres*, p. 474; Chiffoleau, "Saint Louis," p. 19.

24 Cheyette, "Royal Safeguard in Medieval France," p. 640. For a valuable corrective to Cheyette's pessimism, see Shaul, *Prince and the Priors*, pp. 159, 170–88.

25 *Actes du Parlement de Paris*, 1:32 no. 365; *Olim*, 1:454–5 no. xviii.

flict, wished to resolve it, and was even willing to leave the matter to binding arbitration by delegates he and the archbishop could agree on, for the monastery and the crown stood together in opposition to the archbishop's claim.[26] While surviving references to this case are plentiful, they are not always specific or comprehensive as to the people on the ground who were making investigations, collecting depositions, and arbitrating the dispute. Tillemont did have access to some information on these points and noted two arbiters chosen to end the dispute in the midst of the long-running proceedings. These were Jean of Troyes, who was the non-resident archdeacon of Bayeux, and a certain Philippe, whom he identified as the *théologal* of Bayeux, a now archaic term he employed to translate *scholasticus*, the title of the holder of the prebend at the cathedral there who had the instruction of students attached to it.[27] This, as we know, was Philippe of Cahors.

Archbishop Thomas must have had faith in Philippe's integrity, since Thomas agreed to the latter's role in the arbitration. Perhaps he regarded their long acquaintance in Reims as a positive factor. Of course, the king must already have learned to trust Philippe's instincts and to have confidence that he would render a just judgment, even though an otherwise neutral observer might consider the clerk's earlier service in Reims grounds for disqualification. (Resort to people with reputations for evenhandedness, even when their pre-existing familiarity with the parties might make them suspect, has been documented elsewhere.)[28] In any case, if the two arbiters proved unable to reach accord on aspects of the dispute, Eudes Rigaud, the Franciscan archbishop of Rouen, was to take over, and he was to have the decisive voice.[29] The fallback arbiter, Archbishop Eudes, was perhaps the king's closest friend.[30] In the words of Adam Davis, he deserves the denomination "holy bureaucrat" for both his dedication to the service of the Lord as a prelate and his labour for the crown as a judge of the Norman High Court or Exchequer and as a councillor in *Parlement*; "there was no incompatibility between holiness and administration."[31] However, although he was a royal friend, Eudes had a reputation for defending the legitimate rights of churchmen with vigour, even against the crown's claims.[32] This blend – apparently unshakeable honesty together with

---

26 Tillemont, *Vie de saint Louis*, 4:198.
27 Tillemont, *Vie de saint Louis*, 4:198.
28 Shaul, *Prince and the Priors*, p. 91.
29 Tillemont, *Vie de saint Louis*, 4:198.
30 Davis, *Holy Bureaucrat*, pp. 157–73.
31 Davis, *Holy Bureaucrat*, pp. 30–156 and, for the quotation, 178.
32 Davis, *Holy Bureaucrat*, pp. 133–4.

admiration for the kind of governance with which Louis IX was obsessed – is what one glimpses time and again in the person of Philippe of Cahors as well.

The original arbiters did reach a decision, sealed in 1262. Intentions notwithstanding, however, and as Tillemont remarked, quibbling continued, quibbling made possible by Archbishop Thomas's death in 1263, soon after the arbitration concluded.[33] Despite the archbishop's having accepted the decision, which largely favoured his claims, a disputed election to his office following his demise and resulting in two claimants to the archiepiscopal throne delayed and problematized the effective confirmation of the arbiters' settlement. Further jurisdictional provocations from Saint-Remi's sergeants also complicated matters.[34] All sides provided new depositions in 1264.[35] Indeed, arguments in the case continued into 1267.[36] Finally, in 1268 all the parties affirmed Philippe and Jean's original decision that the guard of the monastery belonged not to the crown but to the archiepiscopal office and the cathedral chapter.[37] Other niggling jurisdictional disputes between the archbishop and the monastery ensued, no doubt bitterer because of this so-called resolution.[38]

Another case in *Parlement* in which a major cathedral was a party and for which evidence survives on Philippe of Cahors's role arose in 1262.[39] Once again in the company of Jean of Troyes, the archdeacon of Bayeux, Philippe heard witnesses concerning a dispute over jurisdiction between the king, on the one hand, and the dean and cathedral chapter of Sens, on the other. The dispute concerned the exercise of justice in matters affecting people who were said to be personal dependents of the crown, but who were living ("getting up and going to bed") in villages that in other respects belonged to the rural dean and chapter of the collegiate churches of Soucy and Véron located in the modern-day *département* of the Yonne. These villages were at the time dependencies of the dean and chapter of the cathedral of Sens. The clerics of the cathedral put forward their claim based on custom. There had been instances in time past when beadles summoned the king's men in these villages to the cathedral clerics' court and answered these summonses there for various misdeeds lumped together in the churchmen's brief as "injuries, debts and other matters." Archdeacon Jean and Master Philippe decided that the proofs, based

---

33 Tillemont, *Vie de saint Louis*, 4:198.
34 Tillemont, *Vie de saint Louis*, 4:198.
35 *Actes du Parlement de Paris*, 1:75 nos. 818C–E.
36 *Olim*, 1:701 no. xi.
37 Tillemont, *Vie de saint Louis*, 4:199.
38 *Actes du Parlement de Paris*, 1:159 no. 1710 and 330 no. 182; *Olim*, 1:863–4 no. xxix.
39 *Olim*, 1:160–1 no. iv.

in custom, alleged by the dean and cathedral chapter were inadequate for a successful challenge of the king's claim of jurisdiction over persons dependent on him in Soucy and Véron. In a formula widely encountered in the records of *Parlement* to describe a definitive failure of complainants' cases, the dean and chapter were said to have proved nothing, *Nichil probatum est*, and the king's jurisdiction was affirmed (*remaneat dominus Rex in saisina sua*). As usual, the formal record in the *Olim* is terse. It is valuable as far as it goes, but one would like to know more. In this instance, one can.

The basis for Archdeacon Jean and Master Philippe's decision reveals itself in one of the original depositions.[40] Archbishop Guillaume of Sens took this once-sealed chirograph or a duplicate away from the proceedings, following the court's decision. It survived in the cathedral archives, now deposited in the *département* of the Yonne. Guillaume was a nobleman of the Brossen lineage.[41] He served as archbishop of Sens from 1258 to 1269, that is, during the inquiry into the jurisdictional dispute over the king's men in Soucy and Véron. In his deposition, he attested truthfully (*in verbo veritatis*) that one Gilles Cornu, a former canon of Sens, as well as other canons there used to collect funds at Soucy to support the prebends they held at the cathedral. Gilles Cornu went on to become dean of the cathedral chapter and then archbishop of Sens (1244–54). In the process, he gave up the prebend and with it the revenues from Soucy. Archbishop Guillaume swore of his own knowledge that Gilles possessed the canonry and received part of its prebendal income in the years after Louis IX became king (1226) but before Gilles became archbishop (1244). Guillaume added that in this period judges acting in the name of Gilles and the other cathedral canons, who similarly collected income from Soucy, were accustomed without challenge and routinely – *pacifice et quiete et frequenter* – to do justice to everyone who lived there. This justice applied irrespective of whether the particular Soucy villagers were dependent on the king's demesne, dependent on him personally, or for that matter dependent on any other lords or lordships.

Why was this testimony not dispositive in favour of the dean and cathedral chapter of Sens and their claim to jurisdiction over the king's dependents in Soucy and Véron? How could Jean of Troyes and Philippe of Cahors assert that the complainants had proved nothing? Two reasons come to mind. The allegation in *Parlement* had involved the villages, Soucy *and* Véron. If Archbishop

---

40 See "Attestation de Guillaume de Brosse," p. 64, for the transcription and a few editorial notes.
41 His tomb effigy is reproduced online: *Roger de Gaignières (1642–1715) – Collectionneur*, p. 42.

Guillaume refused to speak of the situation in Véron – and his interlocutors must have asked him – it was because he had no first-hand evidence of prebendal income being associated with rights of justice over the king's people there. The second reason is that his deposition failed to make a *causal* link between the canons' prebendal income and their collection of judicial fines from the kings' dependents. He described what had happened in the past. He did not say specifically that it should have happened, only that it had happened without incident and often.

The obvious applicable principle here – "a well known doctrine," in Ernst Kantorowicz's words[42] – was encapsulated in the maxim that time did not run against the king (conventionally, *Nullum tempus occurit regi*, but expressed in other pithy formulations as well). What this means is that not even a very long term exercise of powers that originally belonged to the crown could bar the royal right to recover, if there had been no express delegation of those powers.[43] The archbishop, one sees now, made limited points that, strictly speaking, honoured his claim to the masters in *Parlement* that he was deposing *in verbo veritatis*. The very fact that the crown was then challenging the dean and chapter's claim and that in his deposition Guillaume ignored the period between the death of Gilles Cornu in 1254 and his own election as archbishop in 1258 suggested that there was no evidence of a proper and enforceable royal delegation of its jurisdiction. If there had been, the judges in *Parlement* would have discovered it in having their clerks comb through the archives. Consequently, Jean of Troyes and Philippe of Cahors ruled that the dean and chapter had proved nothing, which actually means that the latter had not proved a central aspect of their claim, the result being that the whole claim failed.

"Combing through the archives" – I have chosen the phrase with considerable deliberation, for Philippe of Cahors was soon joined in an important case by a certain clerk, Jean of Montluçon, who played a major role in creating the system for recording and archiving the records of *Parlement*.[44] The case, which I have discussed at length elsewhere, partly turned on the question of available records, and the inadequate archive practices of small "collectivities," like the Norman village of Ézy.[45] Two peasants from the village managed to bring a petition to *Parlement* in 1263 in the name of the inhabitants. They hoped to receive a favourable hearing that would overturn two royal decisions, one, in 1212, going

---

42 Kantorowicz, *King's Two Bodies*, p. 168 no. 236.
43 Kantorowicz, *King's Two Bodies*, pp. 164–6.
44 *Olim*, 1:440 note, 504 no. xxx, and 1024–5.
45 *Olim*, 1:178 no. i. For my study, see Jordan, "Rustics Petitioning to *Parlement* in the Thirteenth Century."

back to the time of Philip II Augustus, the other, in 1225, to his son Louis VIII's reign. The latter had confirmed the first decision in recognizing that the villagers were subject to the triennial *fouage* or hearth tax in the duchy. Elsewhere I have attempted to reconstruct their argument for exemption – and the reasons for denying the villagers' claim under the earlier kings. That two peasants should nonetheless be given a hearing in the High Court was strange. It was strange, too, that definitive royal judgments should be challenged repeatedly. It was perhaps stranger still that the clerks who set the docket would identify peasant petitioners by name, an unusual practice. *Homines* of the village in question would ordinarily suffice. The identification by name suggests that the petitioners appeared in person without professional representation.

How to explain the anomaly? Very likely the lineaments of the case came to the attention of two or three *enquêteurs*, a body of men relatively recently created by Louis IX to receive complaints about the improper exercise of government policies and the malfeasance of provincial-level and local royal administrators.[46] The king recruited many of the *enquêteurs* from among friars and other churchmen as well as laymen who in general shared his own distress at the ill-treatment of the poor and peasants and of widows and orphans. Many *enquêteurs* also served in *Parlement* when they were not travelling in panels, usually of two or three, on their circuits around the royal domain to hear complaints. My guess is that the *enquêteurs* declined to respond formally to the peasants' petition themselves. They had no jurisdiction to overturn two dispositive decisions from earlier reigns, but they could urge the would-be villagers to give *Parlement* a try – and they could facilitate their appearance.

Of course, the peasants were out of their league, even once the formalities were dispensed with. And they had no written evidence to advance their claim to exemption from the *fouage*. Philippe of Cahors and Jean of Montluçon may very well have shared, in a general way, the king's sensitivities towards the disadvantaged, but that was not the same thing as disposing them to indulge a claim that the officials of previous kings had rejected, especially in the absence of written evidence, like a charter of exemption. The words they chose when they rejected the petitioners' request revealed their impatience with the proceedings. "These men," they declared, "do not have sufficient grounds to initiate petitioning for redress, and, even if [the grounds]

---

46 The most comprehensive treatment of the *enquêteurs* and their investigations (*enquêtes*) is Dejoux, *Enquêtes de saint Louis*, summarized in her "Gouverner par l'enquête en France de Philippe Auguste aux derniers Capétiens," pp. 271–302. For some useful critical engagement with her conclusions, see Challet, "Marie Dejoux, *Les enquêtes de saint Louis*."

were sufficient, nothing has been established in their behalf by proof."[47] Philippe of Cahors had a streak of formalism that, as we shall see later, he modified only when the case for mercy was strong. Here it was not sufficiently strong to overcome the formalism.

However, the possibility that *enquêteurs* were responsible for referring Ézy's case to Paris provides a good segue to another facet of Philippe of Cahors's career, for he too served in this role contemporary with his work at the sessions of *Parlement*. The earliest reference to him holding a commission as an *enquêteur* dates from 1258. His colleague was none other than the future Pope Clement IV, Gui Foucois, a widower with grown children, who would soon retire from the royal administration and enter the priesthood.[48] Philippe's association with Gui continued the next year, 1259, when he served on a panel of *enquêteurs* with him and Henri of Vézelay, Nicholas of Chalons, and Pierre of Voisins.[49] The nature of this commission emerges from a later record (1262). The men were to review complaints in the *sénéchaussée* of Carcassonne-Béziers, once a hotbed, allegedly, of heresy and certainly a venue for some of the most deadly engagements in the Albigensian Crusades (1209–29). The region entered the royal domain with the French victory. Many inhabitants still claimed indemnities because of military and governmental abuses from those years and in the years since. The panel of *enquêteurs* authorized indemnities for the complaints accepted as valid by the chief royal judge of Carcassonne, who played the role of the king's procurator. Those whose veracity the procurator challenged, he submitted to the "esteemed" or, perhaps better translated, "well-regarded Master Philippe of Cahors" ("amabilem magistrum Philippum de Caturco"),[50] who oversaw more extensive formal inquiries into them.

Philippe's opinions, based on these inquiries, were not determinative in themselves, although given his developing reputation they carried considerable weight. Rather, he joined with his colleagues, in particular Gui Foucois, for final reviews. They subsequently transmitted their decisions to the *sénéchal* of Carcassonne-Béziers, the chief royal administrator in the province, who gave

---

47 A free rendering of *Olim*, 1:178 no. i: "Ipsi homines non pretendunt sufficientem causam petendi, et, si sufficiens esset, nichil tamen probatum est pro ipsis hominibus," which must also apply to the villagers back home as well.

48 Grandmottet, "Officialités de Reims," p. 103; Delisle, "Chronologie des baillis et des sénéchaux royaux," p. 8*.

49 Delisle, "Chronologie des baillis et des sénéchaux royaux," p. 9*.

50 *HF*, 24:619; *Histoire générale du Languedoc*, vol. 7, part 2, p. 198.

precise instructions to his staff on carrying out the judgments.[51] In at least one case, we have the record of the king referencing Philippe's findings and acting on them by means of a letter to Gui Foucois, who by then, 2 December 1260, was bishop of Le Puy and archbishop-elect of Narbonne – well on his way to the papal throne. The bishop appropriately passed them on to Pierre d'Auteil, the knight who held the office of *sénéchal* of Carcassonne-Béziers.[52]

Besides serving on panels of special investigators dealing with civil matters in dispute between the crown and its subjects in the 1260s, Philippe was a troubleshooter on very sensitive issues of personal and immediate concern to the crown. Underlying such issues were typically disputes about property rights and, though fraught, disputes that could usually be settled without engendering lasting animosity, but in certain instances the confrontations grew nastier. Such was the case with a jurisdictional dispute between the crown and the canons of the cathedral chapter of Notre-Dame of Paris in the last year of the king's reign. The ecclesiastical corporations of Paris kept copies of extensive judicial and related records of their franchises.[53] In December 1269, Étienne Boileau, the *prévôt* of Paris, the highest-ranking administrator in the royal bureaucracy in the capital, challenged a liberty claimed by the cathedral canons, a move that provoked a spirited response from them.[54] True, despite such confrontations, Louis remained very friendly with several of the canons, not least the courtiers Robert of Sorbon and Geoffroy of Bar (mentioned above). Yet the chapter as a collectivity, it would seem, sometimes appeared to the king as more interested in preserving and increasing its wealth than in contributing to the often costly reformist programs that characterized Louis's rule. It was one of the few institutions that provoked him to sarcasm. In its defence of its privileges, the chapter sometimes countered with barbs at the king's apparent failure to restrain his own officials' zeal. Louis was known to react by challenging the chapter on the same point.[55]

This mutual hostility was at the core of the jurisdictional dispute that Étienne Boileau's actions provoked. The matter could have been solved by arbitration (it turns out that the chapter's claim to the jurisdictional power in question was stronger), but instead of appealing immediately to the High

---

51 Molinier, "Catalogue des actes," pp. 166, 193; Delisle, "Chronologie des baillis et des sénéchaux royaux," p. 10*.

52 *HF*, 24:692.

53 Tanon, *Histoire des justices des anciens églises et communautés monastiques de Paris* (with relevant texts).

54 Delisle, "Chronologie des baillis et sénéchaux," p. 25*.

55 Jordan, *Men at the Center,* p. 57.

Court, the canons asserted that the liberty of the church was under attack and responded in anger (whether righteous or self-righteous is impossible to know) by excommunicating the *prévôt*. What they must have been aware of, however, was that, like many contemporary kings, Louis IX had worked doggedly and successfully to get papal endorsement of the view that *royal* officials could not be excommunicated without *royal* permission. The point was that governance would be compromised if the king's subjects were forbidden to have contact with royal officials, that is, before the king could send temporary replacements.[56] If this principle was worth defending when churchmen targeted low-ranking crown functionaries, how much more was it important to insulate an official of Étienne Boileau's rank, namely, at the very summit of the capital's administration?

Louis intervened. He delegated Philippe of Cahors as his agent. Philippe was not a canon of Notre-Dame, but he was related to one, Hélie of Cahors (a cousin),[57] and, of course, he was a close associate of another canon, the theologian and preacher Robert of Sorbon, one of the king's most cherished friends. A man like Philippe of Cahors – a royal councillor, a master of the King's High Court, and an *enquêteur* – besides being well known and not an obvious enemy of the canons, had administrative heft. All the parties to the dispute, including the excommunicated Étienne Boileau, the canons of Notre-Dame, and the king's delegate Philippe of Cahors, soon reached an accord. In an impressive ceremony meant to emphasize the solemnity of the canons' retreat from the sentence of excommunication and the end of their confrontation with the crown, they pronounced Étienne Boileau's absolution and the lifting of his excommunication on Christmas Day 1269.[58] This was the condition or reward (it could be read either way) by which the canons had their jurisdictional claim decided in their favour. Whether they really believed this ritual was tantamount to a promise not to proceed by means of excommunication against future royal officials, especially powerful *prévôts* of Paris, whom they deemed abusive was another matter entirely. One suspects, nonetheless, that Philippe of Cahors hammered home the king's point that their lifting of this particular censure was a pledge of future restraint, and the master's words may have been received with particular attention, even as he otherwise proved his integrity by respecting the canons' jurisdictional claim. For, as remarked above, Philippe had weight, and by Christmas 1269 he was a far greater man

---

56 Campbell, "Attitude of the Monarchy toward the Use of Ecclesiastical Censures," pp. 553–4.
57 Jordan, "Philippe of Cahors; Or, What's in a Name?"
58 Delisle, "Chronologie des baillis et des sénéchaux," p. 25*.

than all the descriptions of him as court councillor, *parlementaire,* and fact-finder/judge on special assignment can convey. He had become, as we shall now see, the king's administrative alter ego, a circumstance that must also have played a noteworthy role in bringing the canons of Notre-Dame to concur in the lifting of Étienne Boileau's excommunication.

CHANCELLOR IN ALL BUT NAME

The formal position that Philippe of Cahors came to hold in the royal administration was known as guard or keeper of the seal.[59] Louis IX had appointed him to this position by December 1263 or perhaps as early as 1261. In either case, the clerk's rise was meteoric.[60] In the absence of a chancellor, an office kept vacant intermittently before the reign of Louis IX and continuously thereafter until 1314, the guard of the royal seal was chancellor in all but name and therefore the highest administrator of the realm.[61] It was, in Robert Fawtier's words, "unthinkable that [the Capetians] should suppress the great offices of state, which had been handed down from the Carolingian emperors, and were in their own eyes indispensable to the royal prestige and dignity. They solved the difficulty not by extinguishing the great offices but by appointing nonentities to some of them and leaving those of seneschal and chancellor vacant."[62] The avoidance of the title "chancellor" was, in other words, deliberate policy. Most alarmingly, the twelfth century had seen both the rise of the Garland family and, through Étienne de Garland's possession of the chancellorship, a concentration of power that Philip II perceived as a threat to his own. *Data cancellaria vacante* became the usual formula attached to royal diplomas as the king experimented with delaying appointments.

This terminological legerdemain did not prevent observers from recognizing where the traditional powers of the chancellor resided, namely, in the guard of the seal. Moreover, as the memory of the Garland danger faded, commentators on occasion casually attributed the greater title to the man keeping the seal. In a letter of Pope Urban IV of 18 December 1263, the pontiff, for example, expressly referred to Philippe of Cahors as chancellor, presumably because he thought the custody and use of the seal essentially bestowed the chancellorship

---

59 Perrichet, *Grande chancellerie,* p. 296.
60 Perrichet, *Grande chancellerie,* p. 171.
61 Grandmottet, "Officialités de Reims," p. 103; Fawtier, *Capetian Kings of France,* p. 173.
62 Fawtier, *Capetian Kings of France,* p. 172; Baldwin, *Government of Philip Augustus,* pp. 34, 116, 404.

on the royal clerk.[63] After all, as Léopold Delisle and Lucien Perrichet put it, the work Philippe did was comparable to that of the men who once bore the formal title.[64] Was the pope personally in a position to know and fully appreciate how his usage contravened "official" royal policy? True, Jacques Pantaléon, the future Urban IV, was French by birth (circa 1195) but originally from Troyes, the capital of Champagne. Despite his being educated in Paris, whether he had any real knowledge of contemporary royal preferences with regard to nomenclature in secular government might be doubted.

At any rate, the future pope's career would not have induced him to stay abreast of internal conversations about what one could call officials in the table of ranks, to borrow a later Russian imperial phrase, in Parisian government service. Jacques Pantaléon's eyes looked eastward. He first earned a reputation as an expert in German affairs. Beginning in 1253 he served as bishop of Verdun, a see located in the geographical march between France and the empire. It was dependent on the ecclesiastical province of Trier, not on a French archdiocese. Two years later, in 1255, Jacques assumed the position of patriarch of Jerusalem. However, owing to the realities of politics in Outremer, with the Holy City then being in Muslim hands, his "promotion" did not necessarily foretell his physical relocation to the eastern Mediterranean. What his new job did necessitate was that he focus most of his attention on southern European affairs, a conceptual turn southward even more pronounced after he became pope in 1261. In other words, Urban IV's reference to Philippe of Cahors as chancellor was either a sensible guess, a momentary lapse in protocol (possibly with him or his scribes preferring not to obfuscate), or a simple error based on ignorance. Whatever the case, it was trivial. Even without a chancellor by title in France, the work of the French chancery had to be done, and Philippe had supervision of it in 1263 and continued to have it for some years to come.

Two years later and more characteristically, Alphonse of Poitiers, the king's brother, who, ruling his territories from Paris, was intimately cognizant of administrative protocols in the court of Louis IX, avoided referring to Philippe of Cahors as chancellor. On 28 November 1265 he or a clerk of his in his name had formally requested from Philippe the latter's intervention to expedite the resolution of a conflict involving one of Alphonse's vassals (*fidelis*), a knight by the name of Robert de Saint Clair.[65] The same request was made at just about the same time by Alphonse directly to the king himself, as if the count

---

63 Perrichet, *Grande chancellerie*, p. 171.
64 Delisle, "Chronologie des baillis et des sénéchaux royaux," p. 26* no. 18; Perrichet, *Grande chancellerie*, p. 171.
65 *Correspondance administrative*, 2:500 no. 1956; Perrichet, *Grande chancellerie*, p. 171.

recognized that Philippe was serving as the formal receiver of the petition and could act at the king's pleasure in response.[66] This seems like the role of a *cancellarius regis*, not merely that of a clerk (*regis Francie clericus*) or keeper of the seal. However, the fiction was maintained. In 1268, in two other instances, it was no different. A record (a scribally careless *procès-verbal*) of the homage that the king's son Jean, the count of Nevers, rendered to Étienne Tempier, the bishop of Paris, referred to the guard of the seal with his simplest of titles, Master Philippe of Cahors (*Magister Philippus de Catreco*, recte *Caturco*).[67] Whatever his role might have been at the ceremony, Philippe's title does not appear in the record as *cancellarius*. Nor is he designated other than as *magister* in the reception by the King's Council of the delegation of the cathedral chapter of Paris for permission to elect Étienne bishop at the same time.[68]

The avoidance of the word, however, was interrupted probably with good cause in a letter dated 20 June 1269. The writer, none other than Alphonse of Poitiers or one of his clerks, expressly addressed the recipient, Master Philippe of Cahors, as the king's chancellor (*regis cancellarius*). In the body of the text the count signified to the *magister* that a royal clerk who was also subdeacon of the cathedral of Chartres had resolved a dispute between himself (Alphonse) and the bishop of Cahors (relevant records were dutifully copied into the letter).[69] Of course, Alphonse and his officials and all those in the royal court knew that Philippe was not formally the high officer of state. Yet it may have been considered prudent to differentiate the status of the different royal clerks referred to in the letter by identifying Philippe as the "king's chancellor." Or should the phrase be translated less loftily as "royal chancery [clerk]"? It is a good question. An answer – namely, no – might lie in the potentiality that people were anticipating Philippe's receiving the formal title, as Louis IX made the final arrangements for government in his absence on crusade, including naming two men, Simon de Nesle, lord of Clermont, and Mathieu of Vendôme, the abbot of Saint-Denis, as co-regents. Even though one knows in hindsight that the chancellorship was destined to remain vacant for almost another half

---

66 *Correspondance administrative*, 2:500 no. 1955.
67 *Cartulaire de l'église Notre Dame de Paris*, 1:171; Delisle, "Chronologie des baillis et des sénéchaux royaux," p. 26* no. 18. Also present as witnesses to this homage, according to the *procès-verbal*, were another of Louis's sons, Pierre, and the *prévôt* of Paris, Étienne Boileau (*dictus Boiliaue*).
68 *HF*, 24, "Preuves de la Préface," p. 332* no. 162.
69 *Correspondance administrative*, 2:171 no. 1467; *HF*, 24, "Chronologie des baillis et des sénéchaux," p. 26* no. 18. I do not know whether it is anything more than fortuitous that the resolution of a dispute involving the bishop of Cahors was received by a clerk of Cahorsin birth.

century, in the year 1269 it would not have been surprising if any number of Parisian administrators thought the future would be otherwise and looked forward expectantly to Philippe's job title being enhanced specifically for the period of the regency. Their expectation, if I am correct, proved mistaken, but that was because Philippe was in line for a potentially even more exalted position. If Mathieu of Vendôme died or was incapacitated while Louis IX was on crusade or for some reason resigned the co-regency, it was Philippe of Cahors who was to assume his office.[70]

---

70 *Ordonnances*, 11:lxxxii; Tillemont, *Vie de saint Louis*, 5:130; Fisquet, *France pontificale*, 8:29; Grandmottet, "Officialités de Reims," p. 103; Goetzmann de Thune, *Essais*, p. 79; Hélary, *La dernière croisade*, p. 82. Simon de Nesle's backup was Jean de Nesle, count of Ponthieu.

3

BISHOP OF ÉVREUX

Évreux would become the capital of a separate county in Normandy in 1307,[1] but until then it was under the unmediated lordship of the French crown. In practice, the bishopric was in the king's gift in the thirteenth century. In the year 1269, the see became vacant with the death of Raoul of Chevry, the successor in 1263 of Raoul Grosparmi of Périers. Grosparmi, who was keeper of the seal in the 1250s (and in rapid hindsight regarded as *cancellarius*)[2] until his assumption of the bishopric of Évreux in 1259, had moved on to a different phase of his career as a cardinal and papal legate,[3] a path similar to one that Raoul of Chevry might otherwise have anticipated but for his demise. Louis IX first offered the vacant bishopric to his friend and confidant Mathieu of Vendôme, the abbot of Saint-Denis. The king probably thought that being a bishop rather than an abbot was more appropriate for a monk he intended to elevate to the regency. Of course, the monastery of Saint-Denis had prestige beyond that of most bishoprics in France, and there was the example of the co-regency of Abbot Suger of Saint-Denis during King Louis VII's absence on the Second Crusade.[4] When the very sedentary abbot declined to stand for election to the see of Évreux,[5] the king nonetheless maintained himself in his determination to have Mathieu serve as co-regent. It also seems to have struck Louis that perhaps his friend thought Évreux was too great a step down from the headship of Saint-Denis, but the abbot also declined the far more

---

1 Charon, *Princes et principautés ... l'exemple de la principauté d'Évreux.*
2 "Majus chronicon lemovicense," p. 776; Perrichet, *Grande chancellerie*, pp. 169–70.
3 Montaubin, "Raoul Grosparmi," pp. 437–8.
4 Park, *Papal Protection and the Crusader*, pp. 112–30.
5 Tillemont, *Vie de saint Louis*, 5:125; Fisquet, *France pontificale*, 8:29; Chassant and Sauvage, *Histoire des évêques d'Évreux*, p. 75.

prestigious archiepiscopal see of Tours, according to a report ("it is said") to which Tillemont had access.[6] The archbishop there did not die until the next year, but may have been so sick in late 1269 that he sought to retire.[7] With the failure of Tours and Évreux to draw Mathieu away from Saint-Denis, the posts went to other candidates. In the case of Évreux, the cathedral chapter turned with Louis IX's consent and encouragement to Philippe of Cahors.[8] That he was guard of the seal and regarded as chancellor at the time was uncannily reminiscent of Raoul Grosparmi's career. He was duly elected in late 1269,[9] and two confirmations ensued, the first from Eudes Rigaud, who as archbishop of Rouen became Philippe's ecclesiastical superior, and the second from the man who secured his election, the king.[10]

As far as one can tell, at the time of his election, Philippe knew Normandy only superficially. In *Parlement* his investigation of cases of Norman provenance, like the dispute over the *fouage* of Ézy, provided him some insight into local problems and attitudes. What he learned from Ézy's complaint did not give him an admiring impression of Norman peasants' familiarity with the law or the norms of good recordkeeping. Now he would know the duchy first hand, including its wonderful agricultural productivity and its mercurial weather that could rapidly change from warm and breezy to cold and blustery, even in high summer. At least, residents of Évreux and the Évrecin region, which was well inland, did not have to endure with the same frequency the heavy bone-chilling mists off the Channel that so often beset the coastal towns.

Philippe's sojourn in Évreux would be a long one. Elected in late 1269, he remained bishop from his enthronement in February 1270 until August 1281.[11] The obligations of a *resident* bishop combined with the distance of Évreux from Paris rendered the simultaneous exercise of the episcopate and Philippe's duties as guard of the seal, with the responsibilities of the chancellor, impossible in the long term. The steps leading to the giving up of these duties can be mapped with great precision. Although Philippe resigned the several benefices he held that provided his salary as a royal administrator, he did not cede the seal immediately after his election as bishop. Indeed, as part of the transition to the regency government, the king formally revested him with the seal in

6 Tillemont, *Vie de saint Louis*, 5:125.

7 Bourassé, *Touraine*, p. 291.

8 Fisquet, *France pontificale*, 8:29.

9 Le Brasseur, *Histoire civile et ecclésiastique du comté d'Évreux*, p. 199.

10 Chassant and Sauvage, *Histoire des évêques d'Évreux*, p. 75.

11 *Trésor de chronologie*, col. 1421; Grandmottet, "Officialités de Reims," p. 103.

conjunction with his naming of the co-regents in 1269.[12] Even after his confirmation as bishop in February 1270, Philippe continued to serve the crown in his former capacity for several weeks, as a reference in a royal record of March of that year establishes.[13] But coinciding with the king's departure from Paris, a new guard of the seal, Guillaume of Rampillon, archdeacon of Paris, was in office by April 1270.[14] The appointment of the latter also relieved the new bishop of Évreux of the heavy obligation, with which Louis had tasked him, of overseeing the collection of ecclesiastical revenues for the crusade.[15] This assignment, however, did not go to the new guard of the seal. Instead, and testifying to the king's regard for the incoming co-regent, Louis transferred the charge to Abbot Mathieu.[16] Delivered from the duty of high administrative office, Philippe of Cahors could now devote the bulk of his time to being a bishop, although with the knowledge that at any time he might need to relocate to Paris to step in for Abbot Mathieu and share the governance of the realm.

As was the case with his new bishop, so it was with Louis IX himself. February and March were transitional months. At this time, besides working assiduously to bring his preparations for the crusade to fruition and travelling widely to bid his subjects farewell,[17] the king arranged for the execution of his testament, in case he died on the expedition. To this end, in February he created a council of men to see to the distribution of bequests. It included a number of distinguished churchmen who doubled as royal administrators and advisers: of course, Philippe of Cahors, but also two of his old collaborators in *Parlement* and on panels of *enquêteurs*, Henri of Vézelay and Jean of Troyes; the bishop of Paris, Étienne Tempier; the archbishop of Rouen, Eudes Rigaud; the abbot of Royaumont, Robert (II); and two royal chaplains to serve as almoners.[18]

The testamentary arrangements were wise, for the regency was short. The ailing king died on 25 August 1270, during the siege of Tunis, less than six months after he departed France.[19] Urgent messages conveyed to Paris from the crusaders' camp transmitted a number of instructions that scholars have

---

12 *Trésor de chronologie*, col. 2171.
13 Perrichet, *Grande chancellerie*, p. 172.
14 Perrichet, *Grande chancellerie*, p. 172.
15 Claverie, "Un exemple de transfert logistique," p. 479.
16 Claverie, "Un exemple de transfert logistique," p. 479.
17 Hélary, *La dernière croisade*, pp. 74–7.
18 Grandmottet, "Officialités de Reims," p. 103; Tillemont, *Vie de saint Louis*, 5:118; Félibien, *Histoire de la ville de Paris*, 1:423; Chassant and Sauvage, *Histoire des évêques d'Évreux*, p. 76; Fisquet, *France pontificale*, 8:29.
19 Hélary, *La dernière croisade*, pp. 6–11.

variously interpreted.[20] What they all agree upon is that the most important order came from the new ruler, Philip III, Louis's son. He was ill, but sent official word confirming the continuing co-regency of Lord Simon de Nesle and Abbot Mathieu of Saint-Denis until his return. The extension of their mandate lasted only a few more months, however. After the new king's uncle, his father's brother Charles of Anjou, wrapped up the military campaign by imposing a financially punitive treaty on the bey of Tunis in return for the crusaders' withdrawal, King Philip and his entourage made their way back to Paris with his father's bones. Simultaneously, the new ruler ratified the council of men, including the bishop of Évreux, who were to oversee the execution of the old king's testamentary bequests.

Mindful of his recent illness, the new king also arranged who would exercise what roles in government if he died. By his testament, prepared in the camp at Carthage 1 October 1270, he named Philippe of Cahors as one of his own testamentary executors.[21] He also added his younger brother Pierre to the group of administrators, stipulating that if he (Philip III) died before his eldest son reached the age of fourteen, a succession of great men, depending on their capacity, were in line for various other posts in the regency. This list included Lord Simon de Nesle; Eudes Rigaud; Philip III's brother, Pierre, count of Alençon; Étienne Tempier; and Philippe of Cahors.[22] In the event, the young king regained his health, and there was nothing more for this group of men to do but see to the proper execution of the late king's testament.

ÉVREUX: FIRST IMPRESSIONS

Meanwhile, the bishop of Évreux, still feeling his way among unfamiliar people and places, was beginning to accustom himself to life in his new surroundings. An elaborate ritual accompanied a bishop's initial entry into the city. As Louis Debidour noted, no text survives that explicitly establishes that this ritual dates from before the fifteenth century.[23] Nonetheless, there are other grounds

---

20 For details on the description in the remainder of this paragraph, see Tillemont, *Vie de saint Louis*, 5:119, 130, 285; Fisquet, *France pontificale*, 8:29; Chassant and Sauvage, *Histoire des évêques d'Évreux*, p. 76; and Le Brasseur, *Histoire civile*, p. 199.

21 Fisquet, *France pontificale*, 8:29.

22 Tillemont, *Vie de saint Louis*, 5:119, 130, 285; Fisquet, *France pontificale*, 8:29; Chassant and Sauvage, *Histoire des évêques d'Évreux*, p. 76; Mien-Péon, *Le canton de Rozoy-sur-Serre*, p. 155; Porée, *Histoire des évêques d'Évreux*, p. 76; Goetzmann de Thune, *Essais historiques sur le sacre et couronnement des rois de France*, pp. 61, 79–80.

23 Debidour, *Essai sur l'histoire de l'abbaye bénédictine de Saint-Taurin*, pp. 137–8. See also Turner, *Account of a Tour in Normandy*, 2:75.

for believing it was already in place in the thirteenth, not least the fact that similar rituals were played out at the entries of other northern French bishops. Each new bishop of Troyes, for example, "rode on a mule to the convent [of Notre-Dame-aux-Nonnains], where he slept that night. The next day the abbess dressed him with his cape, miter, and cross before escorting him to the cathedral, where she announced to the chapter: 'Voilà, I present you your bishop.'"[24] Probably Philippe of Cahors spent his first night in Évreux at the nearby Benedictine abbey of Saint-Taurin, named after the first bishop of the city. This Taurin had died in the early fifth century, and his holy body rested in the monastic precincts. The saint, according to his legends, physically battled the devil and actually polled one of his horns during a fierce encounter. The dislodged horn, its contact with the holy man having purified it, was kept in the cathedral crypt, and for centuries parents pointed to it to frighten boisterous and other naughty children into good comportment.[25] After his night's sleep at Saint-Taurin, the bishop would join in a symbolic procession from the abbey to the cathedral. Monks completed their role in the procession when they delivered him to the parvis and then made the return trip to Saint-Taurin. The dean of the cathedral chapter and the canons would welcome the new bishop to his church.[26]

Thereafter, the community with which the bishop regularly interacted was that of the cathedral canons, not the monks of Saint-Taurin, as even the similarity of the bishop's and the chapter's heraldry suggests. On his seal Philippe appeared, as his recent predecessors had, in his chasuble, with cross and mitre and flanked on each side by the fleur-de-lys. The legend read *Sigillum Philippi Dei Gratia Ebroicensis Episcopi*. Appropriately for a church that, like most cathedrals,[27] was dedicated to Mary, the counterseal depicted the Virgin with Child and the legend *Ave Maria Gratia Plena*.[28] Emphasizing the compatibility, comparability, and desired comity between the bishop and the canons, the chapter's arms echoed the episcopal seal by representing the Virgin and Child, flanked by fleurs-de-lys on either side.[29]

There were thirty-one canons of the cathedral of Évreux in the mid-thirteenth century, serving the altars and exercising the prebendal offices,

24 Evergates, *Marie of France*, p. 39.
25 Turner, *Account of a Tour in Normandy*, 2:72.
26 Debidour, *Essai sur l'histoire de l'abbaye bénédictine de Saint-Taurin*, pp. 137–8. See also Turner, *Account of a Tour in Normandy*, 2:75. Cf. "Ancien coutumier de l'église cathédrale d'Évreux," pp. 185–90.
27 Fulton Brown, *Mary and the Art of Prayer*, p. 16.
28 Le Brasseur, *Histoire civile et ecclésiastique du comté d'Évreux*, p. 201.
29 Avril, *Les archives héraldiques d'Évreux*, p. 74.

a figure comparable to that in several of the other six Norman cathedral churches.[30] At Évreux all appear to have been resident. The number exceeded the sixteen in Coutances and Sées and the twenty-five in Avranches; it precisely matched the thirty-one in Lisieux but fell short of the thirty-six in Rouen (based on an earlier thirteenth-century figure) and the fifty in Bayeux, some of whom were non-resident, like Philippe while he served in *Parlement*.[31] Besides the dean, whose office regularly brought him into contact with the bishop, the canons in Évreux, as in the other cathedral chapters, accounted a number of men who, of diaconal rank or not, grew close to the bishop over time: a great chanter, three archdeacons, a treasurer, and a penitentiary.[32]

One might expect that the bishop would not only live in and through this community of canons but also receive elaborate formal obsequies from it on his death. Tradition, however, had it otherwise. Most of the bishops of Évreux who died in office before Philippe's episcopate had their funerals at Saint-Taurin, appropriate though somewhat heavy symbolism, since the body of the first bishop, Taurin, was having its repose there.[33] The funeral at the abbey was surely intended as the symbolic closure to the ritual cycle that opened with every bishop's *first* night in the diocese being spent at Saint-Taurin's and the *last* at the same place before interment. This symmetry is what raises the possibility, perhaps probability, that the entry ritual was created in tandem with the funeral ceremony, despite there being no explicit mention of the former in records before the fifteenth century.

The monks of Saint-Taurin contested certain aspects of having the bishops' funerals at the abbey. Obsequies appropriate for a bishop were expensive. By the time of Philippe of Cahors's episcopate, there was already a legacy of bitter monkish resentment at having to bear the expenses.[34] As recently as 26 July 1268, less than two years before Philippe's installation as bishop, they had come to an agreement with his predecessor, Raoul of Chevry, on the matter. The dispute had arisen when, on their own, the monks met the cortege of a recently deceased bishop and would do no more than let the cadaver rest in the abbey precincts for a day and a night. They provided no formal

---

30 Grant, *Architecture and Society in Normandy*, p. 20.
31 Grant, *Architecture and Society in Normandy*, p. 20.
32 Avril, *Les archives héraldiques d'Évreux*, p. 74.
33 Debidour, *Essai sur l'histoire de l'abbaye bénédictine de Saint-Taurin*, p. 138; Turner, *Account of a Tour in Normandy*, 2:75.
34 Debidour, *Essai sur l'histoire de l'abbaye bénédictine de Saint-Taurin*, pp. 138–9; Turner, *Account of a Tour in Normandy*, 2:75–6.

funeral. The agreement of 1268 did not forestall the dead bishop's lying in state at Saint-Taurin, but it abolished the traditional elaborate funeral. This new arrangement and the ritual protocols that reflected it remained in effect in the early modern period.[35] In order to get their way, the monks paid the bishop the substantial sum of two hundred pounds *tournois* in 1268.[36] The argument over funerals was only one of many incidents in the history of relations between the cathedral and the abbey that testify to their rivalry, for the monastic community of Saint-Taurin did not consider itself less prestigious than the bishop and the cathedral chapter.

THE BALANCE SHIFTS

Philippe of Cahors's diminished role in government after Louis IX's death bespeaks a major shift in our sources from governmental to ecclesiastical in excavating the remainder of the bishop's life history. Of course, other records, especially royal administrative records, are not silent on the prelate. It was impossible to be a bishop in France in the thirteenth century without having regular interactions with the crown, generating an impressive parchment trail, and travelling to the capital from time to time. Philippe, for example, either delayed his trip to Évreux or hurried back to Paris to attend the burial of his friend Étienne Boileau, the reformist *prévôt* of Paris, in 1270.[37]

He also remained a master of the King's High Court of *Parlement*. He was less active, but he attended many sessions in the 1270s. From what appears to be a defective summary of one case that he helped decide on Saint Valentine's Day, 14 February 1270,[38] Philippe is known to have sat in the chamber of *Parlement*

---

35 "Ancien coutumier de l'église cathédrale d'Évreux," pp. 193–4.

36 Archives Départementales de l'Eure (hereafter cited as AD: Eure), G 6, p. 76 no. 123. This manuscript, the bishop's cartulary, was originally foliated with roman numerals, but a modern archivist has paginated it in ink with Arabic numerals, and this is the pagination used in this and subsequent notes. The magnificent published *Inventaire sommaire des Archives départementales ... Eure ... série G* ordinarily, although not unfailingly, prints the information that is needed for the present study from the entries in the cartulary.

37 Forcadet, "Les premiers juges de la Cour du roi," p. 254.

38 The date is in dispute. I prefer 1270 to 1269 (n. s.) because of the reference to the presence of the bishop of Évreux, but Philippe was not yet a bishop in February 1269. *Actes du Parlement de Paris*, 1:309, and Langlois, *Formulaires*, p. 14, however, accept the 1269 dating. If correct, this would mean the bishop in question was Raoul of Chevry, who was elected in 1263, died on 29 November 1269 (Avril, *Archives héraldiques d'Évreux*, p. 81), but otherwise *never* appears to have served as a master in *Parlement*. Langlois mistakenly gave vi kalends of March (24 February) instead of xvi kalends (14 February) as the day in *Formulaires*, but he silently corrected this in his *Textes relatifs à l'histoire du Parlement*, p. 225.

with the knight Simon de Nesle (soon to be co-regent); Master Henri of Véze-lay; the dean of the collegiate church of Saint-Aignan of Orléans; Master Colard of Ivry; Master Jean of Dreux (*de Drochis*); Master Peter of Corbeil; Henri of Champrepus; and the knight Julien of Péronne, the *bailli* of Rouen. The cause, without doubt, among many others for which they were in session, was the official registering of royal safeguard of the Cistercian abbey of Beaupré in the diocese of Beauvais. Confirming new and registering existing safeguards were practices communities employed when political conditions were in flux or some great change was in the offing. This was certainly the situation in early 1270, as Louis IX prepared to depart on crusade. Without his guiding hand at the helm of government who could know what might transpire in France? Those who lived through the earlier regency during his first crusade (1248–54) could recall that there had been serious problems during the king's absence, despite his careful plans.[39] More striking still was the fact that Beaupré was the special abbey church of Simon de Nesle, the aristocratic lay co-regent just referred to, and his lady. It was there that they wished to be buried, even in his case, as he later expressed it in his will, in the event that he died on a future crusade.[40]

In 1273, one again finds Philippe ("Mestre Felipe de Caours, evesque d'Evreeues") in Paris, sitting with Mathieu of Vendôme, the abbot of Saint-Denis (and by then former co-regent), the lord of Nesle (also former co-regent), Jean of Montluçon, his long-time administrative partner in *Parlement*, and several other masters.[41] The case was an interesting one. There had been a violent altercation in Senlis, after which the victim of the assault begged the *bailli* of Senlis to do justice on the miscreant, who was from the town of Creil. The *bailli* agreed and executed judgment. The dispute turned on whether he had the right to do this. In terms of location, the mayor of Senlis argued that juris-diction lay with his office, despite whatever quirks there were in the customs regulating relations between the crown and the citizens of Creil. This was why the case was so important. Corporations, like towns, cathedral chapters, and monasteries, frequently alleged special royal dispensations from the general jurisdictional authority of other corporations.

---

39 Particularly difficult problems arose following the death of his mother, whom he had appointed regent; Jordan, *Louis IX*, pp. 116–25.

40 Carolus-Barré, *Procès de canonisation*, pp. 173–4; *Chartrier de l'Abbaye-aux[-]Bois*, p. 344; Newman, *Seigneurs de Nesle*, 1:54. Simon's wife was interred at Beaupré in October of 1279; her husband never got to go on crusade. After acting again with Mathieu of Vendôme as co-regent under Philip III in 1285, he died on 1 February 1286.

41 Langlois, *Textes relatifs à l'histoire du Parlement*, pp. 86–7; Flammermont, *Histoire des institutions municipales de Senlis*, p. 184.

It mattered having records that disproved, qualified, or questioned these allegations, because in their absence the royal dispensation prevailed. A dispute a little later (1282) made the point with regard to the men of Viry (dependents of the dean and chapter of the cathedral of Paris) and their exemption from the jurisdiction of Chauny for crimes committed in the latter.[42] In this case, the crown was enforcing a privilege granted by an early count of Vermandois, whose lands had long before entered the royal domain. In the case of Creil and Senlis, however, the outcome was different. The masters concurred and ruled in favour of the mayor and against the crown. The city fathers of Senlis thought the decision sufficiently important to prepare, which is to say, to publish, a vernacular summary of the judgment probably to establish it in collective memory.[43] Had they not done so, there would be no knowledge of the case today. The clerks who prepared the *Olim* did not include it, or if they did, that section of the collection no longer survives.

The year 1273 again saw Philippe of Cahors in Paris. On 9 August he joined with Henri of Vézelay, with whom he had collaborated as an *enquêteur* earlier in his career, to constitute a two-man panel to resolve a jurisdictional dispute. Renaud Barbou, the *prévôt* of Paris, officially observed the proceedings, since the issue referred to actions taken by his immediate and famous predecessor, Étienne Boileau. King Philip III chose Philippe and Henri, designated as masters of the King's Court, for the panel. Étienne Boileau had confiscated a copper chalice from Thiérry Frision for failing to appear in his court when the *prévôt* summoned him. Thiérry lived in the Paris neighbourhood and fief of Garlande. The canons of the cathedral chapter of Notre-Dame, who claimed all rights of justice in Garlande, protested. The panel on which Philippe served acted as an arbitration board. Even though Philippe of Cahors had been a friend of Étienne Boileau, the canons concurred in his appointment as an arbiter, probably because his friendship with the royal administrator had not prejudiced him during the dispute in December 1269, discussed above, over which he also presided and where, despite the impermissible excommunication of Étienne, his decision favoured the underlying jurisdictional claim of the chapter rather than the *prévôt*'s counterclaim. Their assessment was not misplaced. After hearing the arguments, the two masters confirmed the justice of the canons' claim and issued a dispositive judgment in their favour.[44]

---

42 Poissonnier, "Quelques chartes anciennes de la ville de Chauny," pp. 254–5.
43 Flammermont, *Histoire des institutions municipales de Senlis*, p. 184 no. xv.
44 *Cartulaire de l'église Notre Dame de Paris*, 3:376–7; Delisle, "Chronologie des baillis et des sénéchaux royaux," p. 26*.

Although there are other references to his service in *Parlement* down through the late 1270s,[45] many more documents involving Philippe now arose out of his relations with other prelates and with local Norman aristocrats and burghers. Scholars do lament the loss of many original episcopal charters and other records for the see of Évreux. However, thanks to the cartulary prepared in the fourteenth century and to five other cartularies written for the same purpose on the cathedral chapter's behalf, there is an ocean of scarcely plumbed material available.[46] Moreover, this does not include the considerable cache of charters and similar texts surviving for other ecclesiastical institutions and lay aristocrats that are relevant for contextualizing Bishop Philippe's concerns.

Most bishops had considerable authority in the High Middle Ages, and in general, authority translated into power. There was, of course, a hierarchy among such prelates: bishops owed a certain (debatable) deference to archbishops, archbishops to primates, and all to the popes and their legates (deference and much more).[47] There was one exception with regard to the general power of bishops, namely, that of the so-called titular bishops, those whose sees were *in partibus infidelium*, territories subject to the political control of sectarians, heretics, or Muslims.[48] These titles persisted, because the church never gave up on its dream of recovering the sees. The pope most often conferred the titles as dignities on clerical diplomats, who were typically resident in Rome when not on missions. Occasionally, a pontiff would bestow a titular bishopric on a prelate in conflict with a secular ruler, with whom he (the pope) preferred to avoid confrontation. The translation of such a churchman to a titular see allowed the cathedral chapter from which he came to proceed canonically to the election of a new bishop more amenable to the secular authority, to the pope, or to both.

The exception of titular bishops aside, the centuries were long past when appearances might suggest that bishops were subordinate to any other office, like the abbacy, in the church, a largely erroneous allegation made of the Celtic churches of the Early Middle Ages.[49] True, abbots of prestigious and wealthy monasteries were often *de facto* hard to control, the abbots of Saint-Taurin of Évreux being a case in point. It is also true that papal grants of exemption

---

45 Fisquet, *France pontificale*, 8:29.

46 *Inventaire sommaire des Archives départementales ... Eure ... série G*, p. ii; Lannette, *Guide des Archives de l'Eure*, p. 237.

47 On the offices and hierarchy of the Western church, see Renna, "Church, Latin: Organization," pp. 372–7.

48 For the observations in this paragraph, I have drawn on the information on titular offices scattered through the volumes of the *Dictionnaire du droit canonique*, s.v. "partibus."

49 Corning, *Celtic and Roman Traditions*, p. 1.

from episcopal authority to certain institutions (orders, monasteries, and so on) sometimes undermined bishops' powers. Such grants varied significantly in extent. A few monastic orders, like the Cistercians, Premonstratensians, and Carthusians, and a few great monasteries, like Saint-Denis, enjoyed full exemption, unmediated dependence on the Supreme Pontiff. The friars, the military orders, and a few others enjoyed semi-exempt status.[50] Such limitations on their authority could be galling to bishops, but exemption came nowhere close to destroying their authority. Most monasteries, nunneries, and parish churches in a diocese were subject ultimately to their bishop and faced regular visitation and assessment of their activities, limited only by his energy and determination.

Évreux conformed to this pattern. This does not mean that the exercise of the bishop's powers went uncontested. As they did in seeking formal exemption and semi-exemption, other prelates and ecclesiastical corporations often begged special, if lesser, privileges from higher authorities, including the pope, to wall them off from part of the bishops' interference. Over time, the accumulation of these privileges threatened to weaken the role of many bishops, and the more determined of them fought back. One of these bishops was Raoul of Chevry, Philippe of Cahors's predecessor. Raoul was consecrated bishop of Évreux on 29 July 1263. Less than ten weeks later, on 11 October 1263, he was able to obtain from Rome an affirmation of his authority over rural deans (archpriests, the nominal chief priests among the rectors of a fixed cluster of parish churches) and curates. Those who had entered upon their duties without fully taking sacred orders, he could compel to make amends and specify the deadline for doing so. As bishop, he reserved the right to permit deans and curates to assume the non-resident status that was necessary, for instance, for those who wished to pursue higher study in Paris or anywhere else away from their deaneries and parishes. He also exercised disciplinary authority to enforce the deans' and curates' service – their pastoral duties – while in residence. None of this may seem remarkable at first glance, but the impulse for seeking Pope Urban IV's affirmation of the bishop's powers in these respects received expression in the *non obstante* clause of the bull. In it, the pope recognized the supremacy of Raoul's authority, "notwithstanding," *non obstante,* any privileges to the contrary that the rural deans claimed to possess from earlier papal grants.[51]

---

50 Jordan, *Unceasing Strife, Unending Fear*, pp. 24–5, 40–54, 74–8.
51 AD: Eure, G 6, p. 15.

Philippe of Cahors followed his predecessor's lead when he obtained a reaffirmation of this papal grant from Pope Gregory X on 31 August 1272.[52] The time lag between Philippe's consecration as bishop in early 1270 and his securing of the papal reaffirmation a year and one-half later was not a result of his being less dedicated than his predecessor to conserving his authority. Rather, there was simply no Supreme Pontiff to appeal to in 1270. The church was in the midst of "almost certainly the longest" papal interregnum in its history, 1268–71.[53] Moreover, when Teobaldo Visconti, the future Gregory X, received word of his election to the throne of Saint Peter in late 1271, he was in the Holy Land with a contingent of crusaders, the last combatants in Louis IX's crusade, under the command of Prince Edward of England. The new pope did not respond to the news of his election by immediately setting off for Rome. There were still tasks he had to complete in the Crusader States. Given all these factors, Philippe of Cahors's success at getting a papal reaffirmation of his episcopal authority over his rural deans and curates on 31 August 1272 was very speedy indeed.

NEGOTIATING EPISCOPAL CLAIMS

The matters that took up most of Bishop Philippe's time in the eleven years he served as *presul* or chief priest, as the Latin records sometimes denominate him, of the diocese of Évreux were myriad. These included relations with the crown, provincial and local aristocrats and non-aristocrats, prelates, monks, nuns, friars, and secular priests. Equally if not more time consuming were the efforts he made to strengthen episcopal control over landed properties and associated rights held from him in order to sustain the diocesan clergy and their mission, including the maintenance and, if needed, expansion of the fabric of the cathedral church. Still another matter that compelled his attention was the experience of Jews, of converts to Catholicism, and of heterodox believers in the diocese.

It is perhaps not remarkable that a bishop chosen from Louis IX's inner circle was in a potentially privileged and profitable relationship with the crown in the lifetime of the old king's son. Philippe of Cahors scarcely appears to have played much on Philip III's respect for him to garner special gifts or benefits for Évreux or for himself. It was already customary before Philippe's episcopacy for bishops of Évreux to receive an allotment of game – a boar and

---

52 AD: Eure, G 6, p. 15.
53 Watt, "Papacy," pp. 145–6.

a deer – once yearly from the nearby royal forest at Breteuil. This continued.[54] The king also insisted that the lord of Conches render his yearly oblation of a deer and a boar from his seigneurial forest.[55] This, too, was customary. The whole cluster of gifts from the forests to the bishop also paralleled annual gifts made to the cathedral chapter.[56] In July 1275, the king exempted Philippe and his successors from the right of temporal regalia for property and goods in the bishopric's possession in several territories that a local seigneur, Lord Jean de La Cour d'Aubergenville, had earlier acquired from the royal abbey of Maubuisson, founded by Queen Dowager Blanche of Castile, Louis IX's mother. This concession also included the crown's repudiation of temporal regalia with respect to oblations made at the chapel of Saint-Maur in the episcopal manor of Bernienville.[57] What these repudiations signified was that the king declined his "cut" of the income from the properties during the vacancies of the episcopate, funds that otherwise were a render for the protection the ruler provided while the see was "headless," administratively speaking.[58] The promise had a modest significance for the bishopric, but it obviously had no monetary benefit for Philippe of Cahors. His canons may have liked that he secured the exemption, but it had practical consequences only after he died.

If relations with the crown were universally straightforward and tranquil, those with other groups varied and on occasion were heavily fraught. From his judicial service for Louis IX in *Parlement* and as an *enquêteur,* the bishop was used to arbitrating fractious disagreements. In neither role, however, had he been a party directly, although he kept himself keenly attuned to maintaining the integrity of the crown's legitimate interests. Now as a prelate, he found himself frequently at loggerheads with local notables, particularly when the property and jurisdictional claims of his church were directly under challenge.

Aristocrats could make special problems. At Eastertide 1270, or more precisely sometime before the Friday preceding Palm Sunday (*le vendresdi devant Pasques florie*), just as he had finally been relieved of the burden of being guard of the royal seal, Philippe came face to face with the first of many disgruntled claimants to property in the de facto possession of the cathedral.[59] In

---

54 AD: Eure, G 6, p. 198, and see also p. 193; Blanquart, "Cerfs et sangliers annuelement délivrés," pp. 263–6.

55 AD: Eure, G 6, p. 198, and cf. p. 199; Blanquart, "Cerfs et sangliers annuelement délivrés," pp. 263–6.

56 Blanquart, "Droits de coutume exercés en la forêt d'Évreux," pp. 272–4.

57 AD: Eure, G 6, p. 120. On Maubuisson, see Grant, *Blanche of Castile*, pp. 118–21.

58 Campbell, "Temporal and Spiritual Regalia," pp. 351–83.

59 *Mémoires et notes de M. Auguste Le Prévost*, 2:300; Maudit, *Histoire d'Ivry*, pp. 126–7.

this case, the claimant was a particularly litigious noble, Lord Robert d'Ivry, or at least this is the way François-Joseph Maudit, who studied his interactions with other seigneurs, characterized him.[60] In this case, the aristocrat's pique rested on a solid foundation, for it is not in dispute that at some period Lord Robert had legitimately possessed the rents from several tenancies at Jumelles in the fief of one Gilbert de La Chapelle. In the charter Robert issued on that Friday before Palm Sunday at the close of the whole affair, he enumerated the tenants of these holdings by name and by the portion of rents they owed.[61] In an unspecified way the rents had migrated to the dean and canons of the cathedral chapter, likely through the influence they exercised by their patronage of the parish church of Jumelles.[62] If so, when Robert found out, his distress, as the charter makes plain, was keen. Yet he decided to accept the situation, perhaps at the instance of the new bishop, a man known as an arbitrator, who would play a similar role in subsequent contestations during his episcopacy. Lord Robert did so, he intoned, "for the salvation of his soul," *por le salut de nostre ame*, which is to say, for the celebration of anniversary requiem masses for him after his death. The liturgical season of Lent/Easter, when he issued the sealed charter, was a good time to make such a covenant.

On 22 January 1272, the knight Jean de Bruyères and his sister Mathilde, a widow, sealed an accord with the bishop concerning the prelate's guardianship of her underage daughter.[63] The customs of Normandy vested the girl's guardianship in the bishop, presumably because the widow's late husband, another knight, Jean de Drouais, had held his fief of the prelate. The surviving record that had been brought to Philippe's attention implies that one aspect of his guardianship was being ignored, namely, the requirement that he, along with the girl's relatives in the paternal line, be consulted on her possible marriage. Canon law forbade interference in a legitimate marriage between consenting and otherwise unencumbered adults,[64] but it did not restrict consultations with overlords if secular law required them, at least with regard to potential pledges of those under age. Since consultations could lead to an overlord's or the paternal relatives' strong objections, widows on occasion tried to circumvent the requirement to their own advantage.

When Bishop Philippe learned that the widow Mathilde and her brother were trying to do just that, he cautioned them with a reminder that they would

60 Maudit, *Histoire d'Ivry*, p. 127.
61 *Mémoires et notes de M. Auguste Le Prévost*, 2:300.
62 *Mémoires et notes de M. Auguste Le Prévost*, 2:300.
63 AD: Eure, G 6, pp. 110–11.
64 Brundage, *Law, Sex, and Christian Society*, pp. 332–6.

(or could) incur a punitive fine of one thousand silver marks, payable to him. If Bishop Philippe had ignored their efforts and tacitly permitted the child's betrothal, he could have sued and might have reaped the profit of the enormous fine. However, protecting his rights by preventing the betrothal made for a less fraught defence of his position and successfully prevented a non-consultative betrothal from turning into a future precedent. Imagine if the aristocrat had won the case on a technicality. The matter of guardianship and consultation with Jean de Bruyères and his sister, Mathilde, was confrontational. Its resolution had an edge, perhaps especially so because the bishop, his advisers, or the paternal relatives of Mathilde's unnamed minor daughter – or some combination of these parties – resented the perceived efforts of the widow to make a fait accompli of the girl's betrothal.

Confrontational encounters did not always, perhaps not usually, occur, but they were always possible. Binding arbitration, not unlike that practised in *Parlement*, was therefore a rather frequent recourse, a pre-emptive move on both parties' part to avoid the negative consequences of conflict. Later the same year, on 5 November 1272, a certain Prior Raoul and the convent of Sainte-Barbe in the diocese of Lisieux confirmed a protocol on *déport* owed to the bishop and the archdeacon and deacon of Louviers.[65] The law of the church in force in Normandy at the time with regard to *déport*, though not a custom in very many other regions, stipulated that the revenues of a subordinate office should revert to its "spiritual overlord," the bishop or occasionally another rank, like archdeacon, when the incumbent of the office died.[66] It was a limited right, like temporal regalia. Upon the filling of the office, the revenues reverted to the incumbent.

So far so good, but the law was somewhat more complicated than this simple explanation suggests. It permitted the spiritual overlord to collect the revenues under a few other circumstances, as for example when the incumbent abandoned the benefice, suffered an incapacitating illness, lacked the proper dignity to exercise the office, or was dissipating the income of the benefice in unnecessary litigation or illegitimate ways, equivalent to violating a trust in the modern law of trusteeship. Death was the least controversial of these circumstances. The other matters were open to debate. How long and under what conditions did one have to be away before authorities labelled it abandonment? How serious and/or how lengthy did an illness have to be to become incapacitation? Was the dignity of priestly orders obligatory for this or that

---

65 AD: Eure, G 6, p. 133.
66 *Dictionnaire de droit canonique et des sciences en connexion avec le droit canon*, 1:623.

specific office? How much and under what circumstances did the expenditure of income constitute a breach of trust and therefore grounds for the bishop's exercise of the right of *déport*? The arguments in this case have not come down to us, but we do know the whole matter was resolved by setting the total amount of *déport* at 60 s. t. per year. We also know that the matter never seems to have been raised again. From what silence is worth – perhaps not very much – I infer that the parties regarded this as an honourable arrangement, perhaps even an amicable one.

The next year, specifically 19 January 1273, again saw the bishop and his adversaries resort to arbitration in a question concerning the enjoyment of the right of *déport* over the chaplaincy of La Rivière-Thibouville.[67] The party who disputed the bishop's claim consisted of two men, the knight Lord Robert de Thibouville and the priest and chaplain of the chapel Jean Carbonnier. Both contending parties – the bishop, on the one hand, and Lord Robert and the chaplain, on the other – consigned the matter to the arbitration of three clerics who, given the offices held by two of them, were men of considerable standing. One was a canon of the cathedral chapter of Évreux, Guillaume of Porpinchey; another, Raoul of Thiéville, was bishop of Avranches. The last of the three was a cleric, Jean of Le Val (du Val), a common name making it difficult to identify him more exactly. The point, however, is simply that recourse to arbitration was routine, and there is no evidence that the resolution, whose precise details remain unknown, was ever the subject of dispute.

Other parties, like the aristocrat Henri, lord of Vaugei and L'Aigle, and the knight Jean de Chambray, appear to have carried on potentially difficult business with equal ease in dealing with Philippe of Cahors. In Henri's case, a similarity of outlook probably smoothed out any issues. After all, it was not Philippe's efficiency that first impressed Louis IX and propelled him from service as a mere clerk in *Parlement* to the king's inner circle of councillors. The king's closest familiars were men of zealous piety, men keen to remake society. In Henri, presumably, Philippe saw something of himself. Transitions – in this case, Henri's surrender to his heir of the fiefs he held from the bishop – could be tricky business. Yet the parties accomplished everything about Henri's surrender, affirmed before the guard of the *prévôté* of Paris on 8 April 1277, without further complications.[68] The occasion of his surrender was his recent decision to profess as a friar minor. The evangelical bent of this decision suggests that he and the bishop shared a general outlook on life,

---

67 AD: Eure, G 6, pp. 127–8.
68 AD: Eure, G 6, p. 116.

including perhaps a disdain for the kind of arguments that property transfers often incurred.

Similarly, the apparent ease with which the knight Jean de Chambray and Bishop Philippe reached an accord about a new mill that Jean had workmen construct in the hamlet of Varennes in the parish of Gouville is suggestive. It was on 28 March 1279 that the two men settled their respective rights.[69] Silence is once more equivocal evidence, but quarrels over mill rights were common, especially when the mills were new and when unforeseen circumstances, including unexpected financial injuries to other parties, accompanying and following upon their building could complicate the original arrangements. No such complications occurred in the two years after Jean and Philippe's mutual allotment of rights. If questions did arise in this period, then they achieved resolution informally and, as far as one can surmise, permanently.

Philippe of Cahors came from a burgher family, but that did not make his relations as bishop with bourgeois institutions necessarily go smoothly. A good illustration of this is the difficulties that arose between him and the commune of Verneuil on the succession to chattels of those inhabitants of the town who died intestate.[70] Regional customs gave the bishop extensive rights in successions to property.[71] The question was how extensive. Custom, as the prelate came to understand it, demanded that the chattels of all intestates in Verneuil go to the bishop. The mayor and the commune (that is, those who represented the commune, the town council) of Verneuil deemed the claim exaggerated, since the bishop or the experts in local custom whom he consulted wanted to apply the rule even to those, male or female, who died parentless before the age of sixteen. Yet underage orphans who had inherited property from their parents had guardians, who would not think that the seizure of their wards' movable property was proper – either morally or legally.

It may have been the moral consideration that led the bishop to compromise in July of 1280, probably after his men had attempted to seize the chattels of an underage Verneuil orphan or orphans, thus disinheriting collateral heirs who had been caring for them. Bishop Philippe relented and, with the assent of the cathedral chapter as well, he conceded that no underage orphan, boy or girl, of a family that enjoyed communal status (not everyone was a full citizen) was subject to this custom on intestacy. Thereupon, the bishop withdrew his claim of succession to the goods. The two sides confirmed that the

---

69 AD: Eure, G 6, pp. 112–13.
70 AD: Eure, G 6, pp. 119–20.
71 Cf. AD: Eure, G 6, pp. 112–13.

age of majority was sixteen and settled on the following principle: Only those persons who held property in their own names, those who were full members of the commune, those who died unmarried over the age of sixteen, and those who had not made oral or written bequests in the presence of witnesses would have their movables remitted to the bishop or his successors. Apart from these restrictions, the bishop's or his successors' disposition of assets accumulated as a result of the custom was unrestricted.

By his training and experience as an arbitrator in *Parlement* Bishop Philippe was a likely choice to negotiate problems between and among his peers in the episcopate and between them and their chapters. Of course, some "interventions" were mandated by the canon law. New churches or symbolically polluted churches in the diocese had to be consecrated or re-consecrated, and one finds Philippe carrying out such tasks from time to time. One instance occurred soon after the beginning of the year 1280 and involved the blessing of the collegiate church of Saints Peter and Paul in Lieurey.[72] Another mandated task concerned the primatial see. When the archbishopric of Rouen was vacant, it fell to the bishop of Évreux as suffragan to give the solemn ratification to those elected as abbots during the vacancy. During one such interval, on 8 September 1247, the bishop of Évreux, Jean of La Cour d'Aubergenville, blessed the monk Robert, the abbot-elect of Bec.[73] Such solemn ratifications, however, did not occupy Philippe during his episcopacy, because there was no lengthy interval between the death in 1276 of Eudes Rigaud, who was archbishop when the Cahorsin ascended the episcopal throne of Évreux, and Eudes's successor, Guillaume of Flavacourt, whose archiepiscopate began the same year and lasted for three decades.

Philippe did participate in arbitrations involving the clergy, and they were not always successful. Two bishoprics in particular commanded the prelate's attention: Coutances and Bayeux. In the case of Coutances, the incumbent, Jean of Essey, passed away in 1274. Instead of a smooth succession to a new bishop, controversy arose. If possible, elections, from those of popes to those of the heads of small ecclesiastical corporations, were to be unanimous, a sign that the Holy Spirit was at work in the selection (hence, the singing of the hymn *Veni Creator Spiritus*).[74] In the case of the election at Coutances, one faction within the cathedral chapter was obstinate. In instances like this, recourse to a committee of three canons who could act for the chapter as a whole was

---

72 Fisquet, *France pontificale*, 8:29.
73 "Early Norman Charters," p. 136 no. 27. Jean may or may not have been the lord of the same name (above p. 47).
74 "Papal Elections," p. 428; Watt, "Papacy," p. 112; Johnson, *Equal in Monastic Profession*, pp. 169–70. Also note the unanimity rule in English juries: Pollock and Maitland, *History of English Law*, 2:625–7.

a recommended process. This alternative, too, failed to resolve the situation when opposition arose to the committee's choice, Robert Goubert. The stand-off went on for years.[75] Appeal at last made its way to the pope, Nicholas III, who opted to designate the papal legate in France at the time, Simon de Brion, to resolve the controversy. Such delegation of authority to a plenipotentiary was consonant with the exercise of legitimate pontifical authority. Unfortunately, other business rapidly intervened and led to the legate's recall to Rome. It is possible that he let it be known that he was leaning against Robert Goubert before he departed Normandy, but he did not issue a decision because the inquiry was still unfinished. Instead, on 29 September 1279 he transferred his authority to Bishop Philippe of Cahors, who had been lobbying with the other Norman bishops for the pope to make a personal appointment.[76] The transfer of authority evidently led to some friction over the fitness of Bishop Philippe, who may have had his impartiality impugned. In any case, there was a new appeal. In the interim, Nicholas III died, and the College of Cardinals elected the former legate, Simon de Brion, as Pope Martin IV on 22 February 1281. Seeing the handwriting on the wall and, with Philippe of Cahors himself dying in August, having no further extramural support, Robert Goubert withdrew, and Pope Martin appointed a Franciscan, Eustache of Rouen, to the see of Coutances.[77]

The other upsetting case involved the long absence of the bishop of Bayeux, Pierre of Benais, from his see. He was, in the lexicon of a different age, a blaggard, given to lying for personal advantage and consumed by greed. He was a creature of Pierre de la Broce (in Touraine), King Philip III's favourite, a man deeply resented both by the traditional high aristocracy and by the men who had been closest to Louis IX. Several historians, including Xavier Hélary, Sean Field, and myself, have dealt with aspects of Pierre's dramatic story, some of which needs to be summarized here, inasmuch as it is relevant to understanding the difficulties the Norman bishops, including Philippe of Cahors, felt with regard to their compeer Pierre of Benais.[78] In the eyes of the high aristocracy Pierre de la Broce epitomized the upstart minor noble who enriched himself and his family from the king's gifts, positioned himself as the person through whom one gained personal access to the ruler, and, because he had the king's ear to effect it, rewarded with high office those who did his bidding. This, it was said, was how Pierre of Benais obtained his bishopric.

---

75 Lecanu, *Histoire du diocèse de Coutances*, p. 314.
76 Kay, "An Episcopal Petition," pp. 296, 301–2.
77 Kay, "An Episcopal Election," pp. 298–9.
78 Hélary, "Pierre de la Broce," pp. 275–305; Field, *Courting Sanctity*, pp. 77–116; Jordan, "Struggle for Influence at the Court of Philip III," pp. 439–68.

The situation in Paris had blown up in the middle to late 1270s, virtually a baronial coup against Pierre de la Broce, who was suspected of spreading nasty rumours about the king (sodomy) and his new queen, Marie of Brabant, as to the "mysterious" death of the king's heir born of his first wife. The royal favourite's idea, for the suspicions were correct, was to get control of the investigation of the origin of the rumours and intimate to the king that they pointed to a plot involving some prophetic holy women in northern France. In this scenario, the king was to be encouraged to believe that his wife was manipulating things behind the scenes. The unexpected death of Philip III's presumed heir also raised suspicions. And the future poisoning of the children he had with his first wife, as was supposedly foretold by the prophetesses, would open the way to the throne for Marie's own children. For Pierre's manoeuvre to succeed, the maligners of Marie would have to persuade the king to believe that she was involved before there was a chance for her to establish her innocence. Then her husband might not only repudiate her but also turn against her Brabantine relatives, all of whom hated Pierre de la Broce, the man who saw in their very existence, let alone their closeness to the king, a peril to his own position. In the execution of his plans, Pierre employed the bishop of Bayeux, who owed his episcopal throne to the favourite.

Put in partial charge of the investigation, the bishop bungled his master's instructions. The same papal legate encountered before, Simon de Brion, the future Pope Martin IV, who joined the investigative commission, was suspicious of the innuendo he detected in the bishop's words and remained wholly unconvinced of Queen Marie's complicity and guilt. The failure to carry the papal legate gave Marie's friends and relatives needed time to exonerate her and, indeed, opened the door to them to take matters into their own hands with regard to Pierre de la Broce. They executed sweet and definitive vengeance against the favourite in 1276, forcing his execution in 1278. Bishop Pierre saw the handwriting on the wall and fled. The see of Bayeux was for years without a resident lord. This was the situation Philippe of Cahors and the other Norman bishops lamented on 4 May 1281. Pope Martin IV, who, of course, detested Pierre of Benais from their time together investigating the prophetesses, let the self-appointed exile remain in hiding rather than translate him to *partes infideles*, unwilling in his new role as Supreme Pontiff to see an anointed bishop humiliated and his person perhaps violated in the king's wrath. Many years later, long after the death of Philippe of Cahors, the king, and the pope, Bayeux got its bishop back, and he remained in the *cathedra* of Bayeux until his death in 1306.

With the religious of the diocese, Bishop Philippe was usually on good terms. Nothing, however, is perfect, and he had a number of difficult confrontations over the years. With the abbey of Bec and the priory of Beaumont-le-Roger, he found it necessary to exercise his disciplinary jurisdiction in 1275. The patronage of the church of Saint-Crespin of Barc (Eure) lay with the abbey and priory just mentioned, the expectation being that under normal circumstances the appointments recommended for Saint-Crespin would be rubber-stamped by the bishop. In 1275, however, Philippe, following an examination of the candidate, declared him unfit for the position of parish priest. Invoking his prerogative under the canon law, he arrogated the appointment to himself and named one Jean of Louviers to the position in November of 1275.[79]

In October 1276, it was Philippe's decision to consolidate the parish churches of Notre-Dame and Saint-Jean of Morsent (late modern, Morsan) that briefly ruffled feathers.[80] The parishes were adjacent and could not support themselves separately. The problem was that the churches had different patrons who held the right of appointing the two parsons. Notre-Dame's patron was Jean de Sassey, a knight, and Saint-Jean's was the Benedictine abbey of Saint-Taurin. What there was to gain by the consolidation was obvious, a significant increase in the number of parishioners for one of the two churches and, therefore, an increase in the revenues from oblations and properties to maintain the fabric of one church and, by efficiencies, perhaps to better meet the needs of the parish poor through almsgiving. Consolidation would also augment the income of now one parish priest. (I presume the bishop arranged to have one of the two incumbents resign or retire.) The deconsecration and literal deconstruction of one of the churches and any edifices appurtenant to it would also yield income from the sale of building stones, beams, and the like. Morsent was not, at the time, an important location. It would later become a pilgrimage site of some significance, but that was more than a century into the future.[81] Thus, the patrons were not ceding very much influence when the bishop persuaded them to settle the issue of appointment by alternating with each other.

Still, problems involving the monastery of Saint-Taurin confronted Philippe more than once in the year 1276. The monks were involved in a long-standing dispute with a succession of parish priests of La Forêt-du-Parc, and at least one earlier bishop of Évreux had brokered a deal for the lifetime of one parish priest. This was in 1228.[82] Presumably, this arrangement was renewable or subject to

---

79 Porée, *Histoire de l'abbaye du Bec*, 1:619.

80 *Inventaire sommaire des Archives départementales ... Eure ... série H*, p. 153; Debidour, *Essai sur l'histoire de l'abbaye bénédictine de Saint-Taurin*, p. 134. Fisquet, *France pontificale*, 8:29, incorrectly situates the parish of Saint-Jean in Monflaines.

81 Blot, *Notice historique et descriptive sur Évreux*, p. 103.

82 Debidour, *Essai sur l'histoire de l'abbaye bénédictine de Saint-Taurin*, p. 134.

modification if future parties concurred, but every renewal reignited the central argument. Was the appropriation by the monastery of Saint-Taurin of one-half of certain revenue streams (see below) accruing to the parish church justified by the evidence (did it possess it *de jure*) or was the abbey's possession simply an arrangement *de facto* pending a definitive judgment? Village priests were not well off, though not all were as poor as the ones at Morsent. No matter how well off, however, the concession of half of one's revenues in perpetuity from the sources to which Saint-Taurin was making a claim was perilous, to say the least. The list of revenues was long, as Bishop Philippe learned. It included income from altar offerings at the church and from the so-called small tithes. Churchmen and lay landlords reckoned grain a great tithe, but they reckoned peas and many other crops small tithes.[83] The list also included half the offerings in kind: bread at the high feast days – Christmas, Easter, Ascension, and All Saints – and tapers on the Feast of the Purification of the Blessed Virgin, 2 February, also known as Candlemas, and on the Feast of the Adoration of the Cross, 14 September.[84] Through Philippe's good offices, the parties achieved a final concord in 1276, with Saint-Taurin renouncing its claim in return for an annual render of forty shillings to it from the parish church of La Forêt.[85] Not a paltry sum at the time, it would be eroded by inflation to the benefit of the priest and his parishioners by the end of the century.[86]

It was probably in 1281 that Philippe tried to resolve another dispute involving the monks of Saint-Taurin.[87] A secular churchman by the name of Michel of Veillettes, as his death loomed, retired to the monastery of Saint-Taurin for spiritual succour. He decided the time had come to arrange for the transmission of his property. This property included annual rents on fields, vineyards, and cottages amounting to 4 l. 6 s. 10 d. *tournois*, not a huge sum, perhaps half of what

---

83 Viard, *Histoire de la dîme ecclésiastique*, pp. 26–7.

84 AD: Eure, H 753, parchment MS (original, with four slits for seals, the second retains a fragmentary attachment). There is a summary of the judgment on paper and an imperfect (partial) transcription also on paper. Whoever organized the archives at the close of 1784 ("3 Xbre 1784") added a note on the summary that makes it seem as though there was an earlier original judgment of the same tenor on 6 October 1270. The author alleges that he found this reference in a sentence issued by the *bailli* of Évreux's court on 18 December 1627. I am inclined to believe the author made a transcription lapse, 6 October 1270 for October 1276. Debidour, *Essai sur l'histoire de l'abbaye bénédictine de Saint-Taurin*, p. 134.

85 AD: Eure, H 753; Debidour, *Essai sur l'histoire de l'abbaye bénédictine de Saint-Taurin*, p. 135.

86 See the discussion and graphs in Sivéry, *L'économie du royaume de France*, pp. 65–71, 85–6.

87 Debidour, *Essai sur l'histoire de l'abbaye bénédictine de Saint-Taurin*, p. 113.

a skilled workman might earn in a year.[88] It was worth having, in other words, but it was hardly worth fighting over – unless a principle was at stake – and one was, as far as Bishop Philippe was concerned. The rent-producing properties were in the possession of men and women who held them of the prelate. He thought that the alienation of the rents to the monks of Saint-Taurin was impermissible without his consent as overlord. When he learned of the legacy, the bishop moved quickly in an effort to have it nullified. He was right to act with dispatch. Challenges to the conveyancing of property by legacy needed to be made within the proverbial year and a day or else the legatee would become a bona fide possessor, which is to say, the lord bishop would, in accordance with traditional practices (the custom of the *pays*), have lost his right to sue.

Nevertheless, there were complications, possibly arising out of similar legacies that had gone unchallenged. The bishop was lord of the fief from which the sub-fiefs (more technically, *arrière-fiefs*) were held. As with so many cathedral churches, the bishop's lordship existed separately and apart from the lordship that pertained to the dean and cathedral chapter. In a sense, therefore, the dean and chapter were disinterested observers of the dispute. Both the abbot of Saint-Taurin and Bishop Philippe opted for arbitration to settle their dispute. The two men chose the representatives of the dean and cathedral chapter to effect the arbitration, another indication that the bishop's relations with his chapter were not hostile. A true compromise ensued. The arbiters ordered the equal division of the rents between the monks and the bishop.

Within a year or so, however, if my reckoning about the date of these incidents is correct, a new bishop would seek to have this decision overturned.[89] He would not have done so if it were ancient history or no longer a lively topic of discussion (hence, my dating). He offered to let the monastery redeem his half of the rents for a once-only lump sum payment of 50 l. *tournois*. The monks considered the offer and indicated that it was acceptable. As a result, the new bishop, Philippe's successor Nicholas of Auteil, got a substantial sum of money with which he could really do something. The monks, even though it would take them twenty years to recoup the purchase price, effectively reassured potential testamentary donors who held *arrière-fiefs* that they would not alienate gifts that were in part meant to support the saying of masses and the giving of alms for the donors' souls and the souls of their ancestors.

---

88 Assuming 250 workdays at 5 d. *tournois* per day; cf. Sivéry, *L'économie du royaume de France*, p. 138.

89 *Inventaire sommaire des Archives départementales ... Eure ... série H*, p. 152; Debidour, *Essai sur l'histoire de l'abbaye bénédictine de Saint-Taurin*, pp. 113–14.

Like any bishop, Philippe of Cahors, as noted earlier, also had to pay some attention to the quality of life in the nunneries that fell under his supervision. Better evidence survives for the ruler of the ecclesiastical province of Rouen, Archbishop Eudes Rigaud, whose daybook historians have exploited, than for the actions of Philippe in the diocese of Évreux. One of the routine but important duties Philippe had to carry out was the regular reconfirmation of the privileges of female monastic houses on the occasion of the transfer of headship from one abbess or prioress to another. A seventeenth-century register/cartulary that includes a list of these reconfirmations for the priory of La Chaise-Dieu[-du-Theil] of the Order of Fontevraud preserves a record of one such solemn enrolment of a charter attesting the validity of donations of various properties. Bishop Philippe issued his confirmation for the nuns on the feast of Saint Martin in Winter, 11 November 1279. This took place in a formal ceremony at the priory, where both the prioress *and* the prior, the house being double in the tradition of Fontevraud, were in attendance.[90]

Along with routine matters, there were also occasional problems with nuns of the diocese that Philippe had to confront, one of which was the sisters' propensity to accept more religious into their ranks than the income of their houses could comfortably maintain. This was not an issue unique to or even distinctive to the diocese of Évreux. During his visitations of the province of Rouen, Eudes Rigaud fulminated against abbesses who permitted situations of this sort to arise.[91] There is no evidence of Philippe's splenetic discontent, but at least once he perceived a similar problem, as his intervention in the affairs of the Abbey of Saint-Sauveur of Évreux in 1280 demonstrates. There he ordered a reduction in the number of professed sisters to fifty in addition to the abbess, because the resources of the house were insufficient to sustain more.[92] Fifty-one nuns, of course, still constituted a major convent.

More evidence pertains to the dean and cathedral chapter of Évreux, their problems, and Philippe's involvement in them. Let us recall that the dean and chapter together, quite apart from the bishop, constituted a distinct corporate entity, with their own property and therefore their own separate conflicts with counterclaimants to rights in formal judicial proceedings and less formal arbitrations. Although the distinction may have been clear in the minds of lawyers, arbiters, and high-born or high-ranking litigants, lay or ecclesiastical, ordinary people were prone to interpret troubles that the dean and chapter were suffering

---

90 AD: Eure, H 1437, charter 181, pp. 38–40.
91 Davis, *Holy Bureaucrat*, pp. 99–101. See also Johnson, *Equal in Monastic Profession*, pp. 219–23, and Jordan, "The Cistercian Nunnery of La Cour Notre-Dame de Michery," p. 315.
92 Le Brasseur, *Histoire civile et ecclésiastique du comté d'Évreux*, pp. 201–2.

as a general reflection of conditions of the cathedral community, including the bishop. To that extent, a prudent bishop, in order to maintain his own dignity, tried to minimize the strife his chapter had with others *and with him*. One probably cannot know what motivated Bishop Philippe, if he was responsible, to have his scribes register certain records of the "private" business of the chapter in his cartulary, but it may have been part of an effort to create a parchment trail intended to prevent or inhibit future and potentially volatile struggles. Moreover, it might explain the presence of documents like the following in the cartulary. One is a purchase deed of November 1276 describing the sale by four married couples to the chapter of portions of tithes in numerous places in the fief of Boes and the fief of Saint-Christophe of Surville.[93] Another charter, dated eight months later (16 July 1277), is the chapter's lease (short-term conveyance) of one of those tithes to the curate of Boes (parish, Surville) for 10 l. t. per year.[94] Though these documents may have been enrolled in anticipation of potential complications with the conveyances, the bishop otherwise appears to have had remarkably fine relations with the chapter during his episcopate.

THE BISHOPRIC AND ITS FINANCIAL HEALTH

"Prudent," "fair," and "adept" are the adjectives that come to mind to describe Philippe of Cahors's relations with other men, women, and institutions from 1270 to 1281. Yet the bishop's care for the financial health of his see deserves another adjective, "dedicated," and the cathedral chapter benefitted from this dedication. The bishop was determined to leave his church, in the broad sense of the word, on a sounder financial footing than he found it and to leave the cathedral per se in a better physical condition than it had been in when he arrived. Yet insofar as scholars have addressed his accumulation of income-producing property, principally landed estates, they have focussed solely on his acquisition of the barony of Iliers from the knight Lord Guillaume de Courtenay in 1273.[95] It was a considerable acquisition, no doubt about it. Part of the deal was sealed on 8 December 1273 when Lord Guillaume ceded his rights

---

93 AD: Eure, G 115, MSS 4 and 5. The *Inventaire sommaire* identifies what would be another relevant transaction, a bill of sale recording the conveyance of an annual rent of 14 s., owed by one Renaud du Homme and collected by a certain Roger de Berville for a canon of Évreux, Pierre of Berville. Unfortunately, if my reading of the original is correct, the archivist misread 1263 for 1273. AD: Eure, G 76, MS 2; *Inventaire sommaire des Archives départementales ... Eure ... série G*, p. 47, G 76.

94 AD: Eure, G 115, MS 3.

95 Le Brasseur, *Histoire civile et ecclésiastique du comté d'Évreux*, p. 201.

in Iliers to the bishop for 50 l. p.[96] Five days later on 13 December 1273 in a separate instrument the knight formally published the conveyancing of the fief. He instructed those who had been holding their own fiefs from him as lord of Iliers to renew their oaths of fealty and homage to their new lord, the bishop of Évreux.[97] This was the last act in a series that had already seen other members of the Courtenay family, including Robert de Courtenay, sell their portions of the Iliers fiefs for 400 l. t. and modify the homages.[98]

The submission of the vassals to a new lord meant, among many other things, that the bishop had to adjudicate disputes among them and monitor transactions that might in any way compromise his own authority or income. In the late 1270s, a few such instances arose. On 24 April 1277 Bishop Philippe, who was butting heads with Philippe Le Drouais, a cleric, over the payment of an annual rent in kind, two *muids* of grain, from the fief of Iliers to Simon du Mesnil, agreed that two men should establish protocols – the preconditions – for the resolution of the dispute.[99] One of these men, the knight Robert de Musi, appears to have represented the interests of Philippe Le Drouais. The other, a canon of the cathedral chapter of Évreux, represented the interest of the bishop. His name, Bernard of Cahors, is suggestive; he was possibly or even probably, since Cahorsin clerics were few on the ground in Normandy, a kinsman or old acquaintance of the bishop who had entered the chapter between 1270 and 1277 and held one of the prebends in the prelate's gift.[100]

Since it was necessary to develop protocols in order to reach a compromise between the bishop and Philippe Le Drouais, it is fair to infer that the matters at issue and underlying their dispute were complex and far more significant than the value of a mere two *muids* (a few bushels) of grain. This inference is borne out by some noteworthy transactions in which Philippe Le Drouais and other members of his lineage were involved. In one of these, dated 14 November 1277, Guérin Le Drouais, a cleric like his kinsman, received from the bishop 25 l. t. as the purchase price for an annual rent of 40 s. t. on a fortified house adjacent to the castle of Iliers and on some additional property nearby.[101] The buy-out was part of a more comprehensive and concerted effort to reduce the power of the Drouais lineage in the fief, for contemporary with Guérin's sale,

---

96 AD: Eure, G 6, pp. 187–8.
97 AD: Eure, G 6, p. 187.
98 AD: Eure, G 6, pp. 186–7; Fisquet, *France pontificale*, 8:29; Le Brasseur, *Histoire civile et ecclésiastique du comté d'Évreux*, p. 201.
99 AD: Eure, G 6, pp. 188–9.
100 For a list of such prebends, see AD: Eure, G 6, p. 261.
101 AD: Eure, G 6, pp. 190–1.

Philippe Le Drouais conveyed even more valuable property to the see.[102] This time the recipients (purchasers) were two canons of the cathedral chapter, Hélie *de Saruliaco*, the chanter, and Pierre Beraud. The total purchase price that Philippe Le Drouais received was the colossal sum of 2,000 l. t. Guillaume of Popincourt, the dean of the cathedral chapter, witnessed the transaction.

Quite unlike the Drouais lineage, the Courtenay family, which in the person of Lord Guillaume had conveyed his rights in the fief of Iliers to the bishop, maintained good relations with Philippe of Cahors. Robert de Courtenay, the lord of Nonancourt, was also bishop of Orléans, and on 25 February 1279 he formally thanked his prelate colleague for allowing his (the Évrecin) officials to levy a road toll (*péage*) in Robert's name for passage to and from the castle and leprosarium of Iliers.[103] He evidently needed the revenue to cover an emergency. Bishop Robert specified in his charter that Philippe's gesture was a purely gracious act that bound neither him nor his successors in the long term. Two months later, on 8 April 1279, he successfully sought the renewal of the concession (presumably for another two months).[104] No further renewals appear in the records.

Bishop Philippe's and the cathedral chapter's other acquisitions were well planned. The picturesque River Iton traversed the city of Évreux. Not very wide, it was nonetheless a source for parishioners' water, for ducks and fish, and for small water mammals that provided pelts and furs to trim the townspeople's garments. Along the banks of the river, the plant growth was lush and either given over to nature and used as fields for grazing or managed for specialized husbandries. Early in his episcopate, by Annunciation, 25 March 1270, the bishop was endeavouring to expand and consolidate his holdings along the Iton, in particular in and around the parish of Brosville (discussed below). Why so soon?

The earliness of this effort leads me to conclude that Philippe was following advice to pursue an initiative already planned by his predecessor. The campaign was steady, extending over an entire decade.[105] The key to property accumulation was not coercion but taking advantage of opportunities that arose from the sellers' need for ready money or from critical life events, like deaths, sickness, and old age. One can imagine that the transaction on the Feast of the Annunciation in 1270, mentioned above, related to advancing age. Guillaume Peluquet sold an annual rent he was collecting from a piece of property in

---

102 AD: Eure, G 6, pp. 189–90.
103 AD: Eure, G 6, p. 192.
104 AD: Eure, G 6, p. 192.
105 AD: Eure, G 6, pp. 159–60.

Brosville.[106] He received 45 s. t. as the sale price from Geoffroy of Courcelles, a canon of the cathedral. Given the rate of return, the canon would (discounting inflation, which was not high until the very end of the century)[107] recover the purchase price he paid in approximately eleven years, about 1281. Of course, he would continue to receive the annual rent if he lived beyond that date, and he could leave it by will on his death. He was essentially providing himself with a pension. The recording of the transaction in the bishop's cartulary may signify the canon's intent to make the prelate or the chapter the beneficiary – or, more likely, to help provide continuing support for the cathedral building fund (below), which was a high priority for Philippe and the chapter.

There followed in the pattern described at least twelve more sales *directly to the bishop* in 1272. These were of annual rents in money (chiefly) and on occasion partly in kind, including capons and eggs that would have had monetary valuations assigned to them in the sale negotiations. The rents were drawn from lands and/or houses in locations in and near Brosville – Langlée, La Vacherie, Les Roches, Mont Normand. Purchase prices varied from 10 s. to 50 s. for the annual rents, prices that would allow the bishop to recoup his payments in each case in exactly ten years' time by means of the rents he would now collect.[108] The sellers, insofar as their legal status is discernible, were mostly inferior to nobles. One rarely finds references to them as lords or knights or with other honorific titles from which one might infer aristocratic rank. They had merely been subleasing these properties, presumably occupied by them or their ancestors at one time in the past, to others. Now the tenants' lessor became the bishop.

Two pairs of sellers in the year 1272 do not conform to this profile: the couple Étienne Le Prévôt and his wife, Jeanne; and Squire Robert de La Liègue and his wife, Alice. Étienne and Jeanne had subleased a more substantial property, identified as a *vavassoria* in the purchase deed, to an unidentified tenant for a yearly rent of 50 s. t. The bishop purchased the rent for 28 l. t., meaning that he would recoup his investment in a little more than eleven years, a lengthier time span than usual but not by much.[109] Squire Robert and Alice had subleased lands to an unnamed tenant for 79 s. 6 d. t. per year. The bishop

---

106 AD: Eure, G 6, pp. 66–7.

107 See Sivéry, *Économie du royaume de France*, pp. 71 graph 1 and 79–80 table 3.

108 AD: Eure, G 6, pp. 141–2, 144–8, 150, 152–6; dated (all 1272) 13 January, 16 January, 5 February, 9 March, December (*bis*), 31 December (*quater*). See also *Inventaire sommaire des Archives départementales ... Eure ... série G*, pp. 16–17, nos. 197, 200, 202–3, 206–7, 209, 211–13 fols. 71–8.

109 AD: Eure, G 6, pp. 131–2.

purchased the lease for 39 l. 15 s. t.[110] Recuperation of the purchase price
would take place after ten years. This purchase, however, was part of a broader
arrangement with Squire Robert and Alice. The bishop leased them a vineyard,
an additional plot of land, and a wood enclosed by ditches in Brosville the next
year (November 1273) for an annual rent of 35 s.[111] This was not a departure
from the bishop's project to recover the unmediated lordship of his properties
at Brosville, since Squire Robert and Alice would be holding the vineyard and
other properties directly from him.

The years to come, 1273–80, witnessed similar redemptions of subleases at
Brosville and other locations nearby, like Gourgis, Le Nuisement, Les Roches,
and Oustrebosc, all at a rate that allowed the bishop to recuperate his outlay in
ten years. The rents came typically from lands under cultivation, like vineyards
and gardens, from grazing land (the appropriately named *Pré-aux-Bouefs*), and
from houses/residences (*masures*)/tenancies – the wording varied. The records
on occasion confirm the proximity of other episcopal properties, such as woods
or fields, already under direct landlordship.[112] From the beginning, it was the
re-imposition of this direct lordship on the lands whose leases the bishop was
purchasing that was taking place here.

This sustained campaign was almost complete by the end of 1275, although
Philippe recovered a few subleases thereafter.[113] The only genuinely big recuperation after 1275 was that of a bundle of rents, amounting, as in an earlier
transaction, to 79 s. 6 d. t. per year, not counting capons, hens, and eggs. These
rents, in Brosville, once belonged to Squire Robert de La Liègue and his wife,
who had liquidated many of their holdings there and acquired others under
the bishop's direct landlordship earlier, in 1272 and 1273. In 1280, the bishop
redeemed the remaining bundle for a lump sum of 12½ l. t.,[114] an amount that
he recuperated in far less than ten years, indeed, in more like three.

Leaving aside matters in Évreux itself for the time being, the other property
transactions in which the bishop involved himself do not come across as part of
a coherent project of redemption. Occasionally, Philippe bought up subleases,

---

110 AD: Eure, G 6, pp. 133–5.
111 AD: Eure, G 6, pp. 136–7.
112 AD: Eure, G 6, pp. 126–33, 139–40, 142–4, 148–9, 151–8, 162–3, 168–9; *Inventaire
    sommaire des Archives départementales ... Eure ... série G*, pp. 15–18, nos. 181 (garden),
    183–4, 186, 188, 194 (Les Roches and Oustrebosc), 195, 198 (vineyard near the bishop's
    woods), 199 (Le Nuisement), 204, 205 (vineyard), 208, 210 (Les Roches), 213, 215 (Les
    Roches), 221, 229 (near the bishop's fields; Pré-aux-Bouefs), fols. 63–6, 71–2, 74–9, 81, 84.
113 AD: Eure, G 6, pp. 140–1, 158–9.
114 AD: Eure, G 6, pp. 158–9.

but not always at the ratio of 1:10 (annual rent to purchase price). I have documented two redemptions at Bernienville in 1273, another at Sacq in January 1275, and another at Condé in July 1280. The 1:10 ratio held for the redemption at Sacq, 4 l. t. in annual rent for 40 l. t. purchase price, and for one of the transactions at Bernienville, 12 s. t. rent for 6 l. t. purchase price.[115] However, Condé's 13 s. 4 d. t. rent fetched a purchase price of 100 s. t., well below the 135 s. t. one might expect.[116] And the bishop's deal with the sellers, Taurin Le Conte and his wife, for the other redemption at Bernienville in 1273 was a real bargain: the annual rent, consisting of 20 s. t. and a capon, was purchased for a mere 36 s. t.[117]

These occasional redemptions were not characteristic. Most transactions at Condé, for example, and at other villages, like Attez, where there is a great deal of evidence for the vigour of the land market,[118] had nothing to do with the recuperation of subleases and the recreation of direct lordship or landlordship. There were outright sales to the bishop.[119] There were infrequent but occasional disputes over succession and the bishop's rights over the property conveyed (*mouvance*).[120] Here, again, the impression is one of empathy and goodwill. Jean Paillart and his sister Agnes (probably minors) had a claim put in for them in November 1276, as near heirs of Martin Cochet, a former *prévôt* of Condé, to the property of the deceased. It was contested by the bishop, who secured a favourable ruling. However, the Paillart siblings had acted out of good faith or simply been misled/manipulated. They had genuinely trusted that they should succeed to the property and followed the advice they received to sue. It was costly for them to try to make their case. In the aftermath of his victory, therefore, the bishop quite surprisingly authorized the expenditure of 15 l. t. to cover the siblings' expenditure in trying to trump his claim.[121] He would not take advantage of orphans or let them be disabled by this outlay of funds.

The bishop's transactions in Évreux proper most resemble the campaign in Brosville, yet on a smaller scale. The city had an active land market.[122] There

---

115 AD: Eure, G 6, pp. 103–4, 145–6.
116 AD: Eure, G 6, p. 105.
117 AD: Eure, G 6, pp. 137–8.
118 Besides purchases involving the bishop of Évreux at Condé (below), see AD: Eure, G 6, p. 102.
119 AD: Eure, G 6, pp. 101–2, 104–6.
120 AD: Eure, G 6, pp. 108–9, 114–16.
121 AD: Eure, G 6, pp. 113–14.
122 Cf. the editorial remarks on an active family in the land market in *Inventaire sommaire des Archives départementales ... Eure ... série G*, p. 18, no. 235 fol. 87; and for additional evidence on this family, p. 19, no. 237 fol. 88.

were by my reckoning eleven successful efforts (only the successful ones would be recorded, of course) to redeem subleases in the years 1272 to 1274. As one would expect for a city, most of the subleases pertained to one or at most two houses (eight of the eleven).[123] Three deeds mention plots of land, including a vineyard and an enclosure (*clos*), probably also a vineyard.[124] The ratio of rent to purchase price was the typical 1:10. The transactions not only look like a concentrated campaign but one whose goal was the same as it was in Brosville, the comprehensive re-establishment of direct episcopal lordship.

ÉGLISE NOTRE-DAME D'ÉVREUX

In the end, most of what Philippe of Cahors did on the financial side during his episcopate directly or indirectly supported the mission of the cathedral and diocesan clergy. This included maintaining and even enhancing the fabric of the cathedral church. Our Lady of Évreux was always a work in progress. The general opinion seems to be that it was in 1270 that the rebuilding of the cathedral choir in the so-called rayonnant Gothic style was set in motion.[125] If this is accurate, then the first phase of the work occurred under the watchful eye of Philippe of Cahors, who became bishop early that year. Also, if this is so, his predecessor and his advisers had to have formulated the plans long before and accumulated a substantial sum of money to finance the earliest stages of the rebuilding. It all accords with known facts, for it means that the exactly contemporary campaign to recover the bishop's direct lordship and landlordship described above was part of a much broader initiative to enhance ecclesiastical life in the diocese. Explicit testimony to Bishop Philippe's activities with regard to the fabric of the choir per se is lacking. Did he have any of his predecessors' plans altered? Scholars, since as long ago as Jules Fossey (1898), have had to rely on disciplined speculation in thinking this through.[126] What does seem persuasively argued is that the bishop influenced the canons to donate (or, at least, he does not appear to have dissuaded them from donating) to the cathedral building works.

In the 1270s Girard (II) of Aumale, the dean of the cathedral chapter, made a bequest of 100 s. in his will for the fabric of the church ("ad fabricam nostre ecclesiae"), as did the chanter, Clément of Rouen. The execution of the bequests,

---

123 AD: Eure, G 6, pp. 138–9, 144–5, 160, 164–6, 180–1.

124 AD: Eure, G 6, pp. 167–8, 173–4, 181–2; *Inventaire sommaire des Archives départementales ... Eure ... série G*, pp. 18–19, nos. 227, 235 (*clos*), and 243 (vineyard) fols. 87, 89, 91.

125 *Cathédrale Notre-Dame d'Évreux*, p. 2.

126 Fossey, *Monographie de la cathédrale d'Évreux*, p. 43.

known from an eighteenth-century *vidimus*, is dated 1276.[127] The 100 s. sums were modest. If the thirteenth- and fourteenth-century fiscal accounts of the bishopric had survived, they would presumably show that these bequests were two of many similar gifts and of many other kinds of donations in support of the cathedral's expansion and maintenance.

The financial effort to garner support was long term. The construction of the choir alone took approximately forty years (1270–1310).[128] The builders did not complete their work, in other words, until more than a generation after Bishop Philippe's death. As construction concluded, the radiant beauty of the choir appears to have encouraged additional enhancements. Robert of Fresnes, a canon who was archdeacon of the cathedral in the late thirteenth century, founded a chapel in the right-hand portion of the chevet of the church.[129] Progress was slow. A charter dated 14 September 1308, the Friday before the feast of Saint Matthew the Apostle, describes the chapel, summarized as having been "fondez en leglise nostredame devreux," as still under construction, "erecta, [sed] non perfecta vel consummata."[130] Nevertheless, confident that the completion of the work and the dedication of the altar were imminent, Archdeacon Robert also donated an annual rent of 12 l. t. to support a chaplain.[131]

THE CHRISTIAN FAITH

Still another matter of concern to the bishop must have been the conditions of life for the Jews in the diocese. As a churchman, Philippe had no spiritual jurisdiction over Jews. He could not excommunicate them, since they were not in communion. (Strange as it may sound, a few churchmen claimed for a while, beginning in the early thirteenth century, that they could.)[132] Jewish excommunication (*herem*) imposed by the synagogue on "wayward" Jews was not a process over which churchmen usually had any influence and certainly no formal authority as prelates. Nonetheless, it was incumbent on bishops and perhaps on one with Philippe of Cahors's background in particular, in the spirit

---

127 AD: Eure, G 67, MS marked 14.
128 *Cathédrale Notre-Dame d'Évreux*, p. 2.
129 AD: Eure, G 69, fol. 105 v.
130 AD: Eure, G 69, fol. 105 and 105 v.
131 AD: Eure, G 69, fol. 105.
132 Jordan, "Christian Excommunication of Jews in the Middle Ages," pp. 31–8; Jordan, "Excommunication by Christian Authority," p. 245; Shatzmiller, "Christian 'Excommunication' of the Jews," pp. 245–55.

of his dedication to the memory of his friend, the late king Louis IX, to work with secular officials in an effort to regulate – in the sense of to limit – contact between Jews and Christians. Other groups, who did fall under the bishop's jurisdiction as baptized Christians (that is, were subject to excommunication and the other spiritual penalties he might impose), were converts from Judaism and Islam, heretics and other Christians who adopted "superstitious" practices. We shall consider all these groups in turn.

With regard to Jews, the traditional concern was to "protect" the Christian poor from usury.[133] Louis IX issued many ordinances concerning usury, including the famous Ordinance of Melun (perhaps more his mother's brainchild) of 1230 that defined usury as anything above the principal.[134] If effectively enforced, the ordinance would have reduced the Jewish moneylending business to the sale of pledges unredeemed after a year. Enforcement was a high priority, as subsequent legislation proved.[135] It was sufficiently effective to cause widespread pauperization of Jews.[136] Other occupations Jews could take up did not offer much hope of economic advancement, since the king put restrictions on the market for their manufactures and services.[137]

In other matters, the king was also intrusive in Jewish life. He ordered hundreds of copies of the Talmud burned, because of two principal allegations against it, namely, that it contained passages that insulted Jesus and the Virgin Mary and that it commended doctrines that diverged from the teachings of the Old Testament.[138] In a cluster of orders preserved for Normandy in 1235, he prohibited Jews from making contact (literally) with Christians in brothels and (by proximity) in taverns. Suspicion that Jews might lead disgruntled excommunicates astray inspired similar legislation about Jewish-Christian fraternization.[139] This impulse to restrict contact culminated in the enforcement of ecclesiastical legislation to require Jews to wear distinguishing signs on their clothing.[140] To encourage conversion, the king compelled synagogue attendees to hear sermons urging them to apostatize.[141] Those who did agree to

---

133 Jordan, *Louis IX and the Challenge of the Crusade*, pp. 154–5 no. 15.
134 Jordan, *French Monarchy and the Jews*, pp. 131–2.
135 Jordan, *French Monarchy and the Jews*, p. 132.
136 Jordan, *French Monarchy and the Jews*, pp. 154–76.
137 Jordan, *French Monarchy and the Jews*, pp. 148–9.
138 Jordan, *French Monarchy and the Jews*, pp. 137–41; Jordan, "Marian Devotion and the Talmud Trial of 1240," pp. 61–76.
139 For a discussion of the Norman directives, see Jordan, *French Monarchy and the Jews*, p. 135.
140 Jordan, *French Monarchy and the Jews*, pp. 149–50, 160, 163.
141 Jordan, *French Monarchy and the Jews*, pp. 150, 161.

convert often found godparents and, therefore, patronage and protection from among the royal family or other aristocratic lineages. Although converts lost their property at baptism (those who had lordship over them as Jews retained it), they received yearly pensions as compensation, again in line with ecclesiastical recommendations, for as long as they lived.[142]

As this brief summary of royal policies on the Jews shows, the cooperation of "church and state" (an anachronistic phrase, to be sure)[143] was a given in the France of Louis IX. The disabilities and inducements would have applied to the Jews of Évreux, as they would to any other Jews in the realm. The Jews of Évreux, however, were exceptional in northern France in one way. They constituted, as we shall see, a very important presence in the life of the wider network of Jewish communities in the north. Considerable evidence has survived on the Jews of Évreux proper in the twelfth and thirteenth century.[144] In Bishop Philippe's time, there was a synagogue in Évreux and a residential lane where Jews settled known as the *rue aux juifs*.[145] Within the last few years and mindful of the unseemliness of such names to certain cultural critics, the city fathers changed the name of the lane, which is a continuation of the historic and still named *rue des Lombards*. It has now become the *rue David*. The plaque that historicizes the change explains that the two groups from which the streets originally got their designations and on which their residences fronted shared the vocation of moneylending in the Middle Ages.[146]

A Jewish school in the sense both of a building (probably a private residence, though possibly communal) and of a coherent or interrelated group of commentators on the Law (*rabbotenu me-Evreux*) existed, and the latter acquired reknown for its significant contributions to exegesis among rabbis elsewhere in the kingdom.[147] The learning of Évreux's Jews, owing to the eclipse of Paris as a centre of Jewish scholarship, is what made the Norman city prominent among Jewish communities of the time.[148] The eclipse of Paris occurred after and because of the condemnation of the Talmud, mentioned above. The destruction of cartloads of copies on 13 June 1242 in the royal

---

142 Jordan, *French Monarchy and the Jews*, pp. 128–50.
143 An observation iterated at length in Jones, *Before Church and State*.
144 For some of the evidence on the Évreux Jewish community, see Nahon, "Les juifs en Normandie," pp. 32, 49.
145 Étienne Pitoiset, "Recherches sur les rues d'Évreux," pp. 151–2.
146 Personal observation, June 2016.
147 Nahon, "Les juifs en Normandie," pp. 32–3, 44.
148 Nahon, "Les juifs en Normandie," pp. 32–3, 43–4, 49.

capital stimulated the emigration of a significant number of Jewish scholars from the Ile-de-France and from Paris in particular.[149]

In the circumstances, other Jewish communities like Évreux's felt a compelling mission to take Paris's place in preserving the normative sources on which to base Jewish religious life and learning. As with other Jews in France, the Évrecin community commemorated the burning of the Talmud with annual communal fasts, an Ashkenazic practice "during" – and to commemorate – "times of severe crisis."[150] Their writings, of course, preserved Talmudic learning, even in the absence of readily available copies of the book itself. They thus became all the more valuable to what one can call the survivalist rabbinic cultural project.[151] These writings were widely quoted by rabbis elsewhere and were quite influential.[152] Remarkably, a fifteenth-century Hebrew manuscript preserves eighty fragments of the legal (*halakhic*) discussions/decisions associated with this Évreux school.[153] A question remains as to why Évreux per se was so important? Why did many other communities as old and as populous, indeed older and more populous, not quite rise to the occasion? A case might be made to associate Rouen's Jewish community with the Évrecin impulse, but what one needs is a sober portrait of the importance of Rouen's Jews, not the exaggerated portrait of them provided in the one book that purports to assess this role.[154]

What is clear is that the Jews of Évreux had an enhanced heft in Hebrew learning, especially on the Talmud, from the 1240s on, no matter what significance scholars come to assign to other communities. This might be because one particular family – with three brothers – was exceptional. Moses, Samuel, and Isaac, the sons of one Shne'ur (*Seignur*) of Évreux, were *érudits* of the highest order. Two of these brothers also fathered sons, Hayyim ben Moses and Menachem ben Samuel, who were celebrated Talmudic scholars. Moreover, the charismatic writing of these men inspired "disciples" near and far: Isaac of Corbeil, Perets of Corbeil, Yedididyah of Nuremberg, and Jonah ben Abraham of Gerona.[155] What is also clear is that Bishop Philippe of Cahors

---

149 Schwarzfuchs, "Le vendredi 13 juin 1242," pp. 365–9; Nahon, "Orality and Literacy," p. 158.

150 Schwarzfuchs, "Le vendredi 13 juin 1242," pp. 367–8; Emanuel, "Halakhic Questions," p. 123.

151 Nahon, "Les juifs en Normandie," p. 44.

152 Nahon, "Orality and Literacy," pp. 160–2.

153 Nahon, "Les juifs en Normandie," p. 45.

154 I refer to Norman Golb's unpersuasive *Juifs de Rouen au moyen âge*; see my "Review," pp. 437–8.

155 *Savants et croyants*, p. 98.

was not intent upon adding to the burden of disabilities on these or any Jews or in sweetening the inducements for them to convert. The existing program was consistent with the aspirations of most churchmen, and it carried the imprimatur of Louis IX. There is no evidence that Philip III altered any of the parameters of the project. Consequently, there was no reason for a bishop to protest, say, any easing of disabilities, as there would have been if the new king had deviated from his father's policies. The bishop had no reason to doubt that the suppression of the Talmud had been successful, and he had no reason to believe – nor could he easily have discovered – that Jewish scholars in Évreux preserved a fair residue of Talmudic learning that other Jewish writers and readers would have recognized in the carefully prepared codices that transmitted it.[156] Indeed, Bishop Philippe was more likely to think the opposite. Delivered from the baleful influence of the Talmud, Jewish learning, he probably believed, was returning to its roots in the Old Testament. It might even have pleased him, if he had known (and if it were true), that the king's Jews in Évreux could be thought (though wrongly) instrumental in cleansing contemporary Judaism of the alleged fables and false doctrines with which the Talmud had infected it.

Converted Jews did fall under the spiritual jurisdiction of the bishop. Lacking the kinds of sources that survive for the archiepiscopal see of Rouen, one cannot add much that is specific to the Évrecin on the general picture of the experiences of converted Jews in Normandy. In Rouen, the most spectacular case involving a converted Jew in this period touched upon his repudiation of his new faith. In theory, churchmen had no desire to hand a convert over to the secular arm for execution, but contumacy led to this particular apostate's condemnation and execution by fire in 1266.[157] I have not come upon any roughly contemporary similar cases in the diocese of Évreux.

Except for their presence in the diocese, one also knows very little about the experiences of converted Muslims in the diocese.[158] Several hundred formerly Muslim families from Acre and thereabouts, residents and refugees in the city, had come to France mostly in the 1250s, at the instigation of Louis IX.[159] Government functionaries settled them in various micro-regions, one of which was the Évrecin. The few families that took up residence there fell under the spiritual jurisdiction of the bishop. Judging from what we know

---

156 On this point and for a photograph of a manuscript page, see *Savants et croyants*, p. 98.
157 *Regestrum visitationum archiepiscopi rotomagensis*, p. 541. Translation from *Register of Eudes of Rouen*, p. 618.
158 Jordan, *The Apple of His Eye*, pp. 67, 99.
159 On the remaining matters treated in this paragraph, see Jordan, *The Apple of His Eye*.

about some of these immigrants, like the thirteen families in Rouen and its hinterland and the almost twice that number in Orléans and its hinterland, theirs was a difficult transition. The new climate was hard to adjust to, even though the government provided subsidized housing, annual doles of warm clothes, and lifetime pensions. The middle to late 1250s also saw a bad famine in northern France, especially in Normandy, as Guillaume of Chartres reported,[160] some of the details of which this friend and biographer of Louis IX must have picked up from Philippe of Cahors, who would have had access to records on the king's relations with the duchy in those years. Evidence from Orléanais speaks of deaths and flight by a few of the settlers there. The burning of the lapsed Jew, referred to above, probably inhibited apostasy among the Muslim converts, who knew they would suffer the same fate. It is possible, perhaps even likely, that the heads of convert families had an audience with the king when he visited Évreux in 1268 in the run-up to his last crusade.[161] In time, assimilation succeeded.

Louis IX's settlement of converted Muslims in France was part of a larger project or impulse that I have elsewhere called the conversion of the world.[162] It drew on a widely shared and deep desire among Catholic elites throughout Christendom to reconquer Jerusalem, to bring not only Jews and Muslims but also Mongols and other pagans to the faith, to eradicate Christian heresy, and to usher in moral reform of the church and Christian society. Never before the thirteenth century had men and women envisioned this as a practical possibility, unless under God's direct intervention, even if it was a hope. The dramatic evidence of the papacy's commitment to the project was the decrees of the Fourth Lateran Council of 1215 and those of subsequent councils, especially the Second Council of Lyon of 1274. Ecclesiastical historians since the early modern period have known that Catholic prelates, including those who served the Crusader Kingdom, and important lay potentates attended the latter council in significant numbers. Also present were Greek clergy and Byzantine government emissaries, there to negotiate the union of the eastern and western church. However, no official list of those who attended the council survives. It remains in the realm of surmise as to whether even as influential a cleric as Mathieu of Vendôme, the abbot of Saint-Denis, travelled to Lyon, although scholars have assumed that he did.[163]

---

160 Guillaume of Chartres, "On the Life and Deeds of Louis," in *Sanctity of Louis IX*, p. 146, para. 34.
161 On the audience, see the argument advanced in Jordan, *The Apple of His Eye*, pp. 105–6.
162 Jordan, *Apple of His Eye*, pp. 1–20.
163 Carolus-Barré, *Le procès de canonisation de saint Louis*, p. 232.

The same is true for Philippe of Cahors. But though hard evidence is lack-ing, all of the standard authorities, especially ecclesiastical historians, insist that the bishop attended. Fisquet, Chassant and Sauvage, Le Brasseur, Porée, Frowein, and others have made the claim.[164] Each of them and undoubtedly numerous others draw solely on the original *Gallia christiana*[165] – or on one another. There may be no reason to dissent on the point. The compilers of *Gallia christiana* had access to many sources now lost or destroyed. Never-theless, as we have already seen, the evidence on the treatment of practising Jews and the treatment of Jewish and Muslim converts in the Évrecin offers no insight on how Bishop Philippe, if he went to Lyon or even if he only read the decrees,[166] tried to translate them into concerted local action. He did take something of an administrative role briefly in plans for a new crusade (below), one goal of the council. But combatting heresy, another goal, does not appear to have been an issue in the diocese of Évreux, so evidence of a determined attempt to eradicate it is non-existent and, therefore, cannot measure Philippe of Cahors's commitment to the conversion of the world.

Were there superstitious practices that the bishop needed to confront and suppress? Is there evidence suggesting a heightened sensitivity to these prac-tices in 1274 and thereafter as a result of the reform program of the Second Council of Lyon? There were devotional practices in the diocese that smacked of indecorum and scandalized the hierarchy. Many a believing Christian, who accepted the reality of miracles, might still have had doubts, for example, about the devil's horn in the cathedral *trésor*, whose origin story was retold early in this chapter, but piety – in the sense of a willingness to suspend one's disbelief – might have prevented them from expressing skepticism, let alone acting on it. The same pious sorts of people, in whose number one may include Philippe of Cahors as the intimate friend of that most reverent prince, Louis IX, would have had greater problems with a set of celebratory rituals that took place at the cathedral every first of May. A censorious description of these celebrations survives, written by a late eighteenth-/early nineteenth-century canon who had served forty years in the cathedral chapter and had direct access to its pre-revolutionary archives for his research.[167] The notes he made were

---

164 Fisquet, *France pontificale*, 8:29; Chassant and Sauvage, *Histoire des évêques d'Évreux*, p. 76; Le Brasseur, *Histoire civile et ecclésiastique du comté d'Évreux*, p. 201; Porée, *His-toire des évêques d'Évreux*, p. 76; Frowein, "Der Episkopat auf dem 2. Konzil von Lyon," p. 320. See also Forcadet, "Les premiers juges de la Cour du roi," p. 254 no. 789.
165 *Gallia christiana*, 11:590.
166 For the decrees, see *Conciliorum oecumenicorum generaliumque decreta*, 2, 1, pp. 249–358.
167 *Opuscules et mélanges historiques sur la ville d'Évreux*, pp. 149–54.

published in the *Mercure de France*, a fact that assured that they would be well known, since that publication had established itself as "the most important literary journal in prerevolutionary France," covering everything from court gossip to the historical mores of the French in seriously researched articles.[168]

The English traveller, antiquary, and Fellow of the Royal Society Dawson Turner made reference to the notes and their basis in the archival evidence when he visited Évreux's cathedral around 1820.[169] It was these notes as well as others by various antiquaries with access to now dispersed or destroyed archives that Théodose Bonnin, the archeologist and local historian of Normandy, collected and republished.[170] Jean-Théodore Bonnin, who legally changed his name to Théodose because he liked the antique evocation of the Roman emperor, was a well-respected scholar. The son of a notary, he tried that profession for a year before settling in Évreux and devoting himself to classical archeology and medieval history, for which he is honoured in a permanent exhibition of artefacts relating to his life at the Musée d'art, histoire, et archéologie d'Évreux.[171] He rose to serve as the French government's inspector of historical monuments in the *département* of the Eure in the mid-nineteenth century and, in a private capacity, to the directorship of the Society of Antiquaries of Normandy. Best remembered – and admired – for his monumental edition of the register of the thirteenth-century archbishop of Rouen Eudes Rigaud,[172] Bonnin contributed his considerable authority to and confidence in his predecessor's report from the *Mercure* by republishing it.

These May Day ceremonies went back to the tenth or eleventh century, the disapproving canon alleged. If true, then the thirteenth-century bishop Philippe of Cahors observed a so-called black procession, that is to say, a solemn progress that numbered all of the clergy among the participants as well as acolytes, choirboys, and various other groups. From its starting point at the cathedral, as the then existing medieval manuscript disclosed to the canon, the route was short. It took the marchers, who carried pruning knives, to a nearby wood. There, they cut from the early spring growth thin leafy branches destined for placement around the statues and icons in the cathedral church in a seasonal evocation of rebirth. The procession going out, the pruning, and the procession back, despite the prescribed solemnity, were cheerfully festive. The cathedral

---

168 The quotation is from Popkin, "Journals: The New Face of News," p. 146.
169 Turner, *Account of a Tour in Normandy*, 2:73–4.
170 I have used the databank assembled by the Bibliothèque nationale de France, online at data. bnf.fr, s.v. "Théodose Bonnin."
171 Viewed on site, Tuesday, 17 June 2018.
172 *Regestrum visitationum Archiepiscopi Rothomagensis*.

bells continually rang during the ceremonies. The sound was decidedly annoy-
ing when carried on at such length. Over time, therefore, it had become an
integral and fun part of the ceremony to invade the belfries, rough up the bell-
ringers, and drag them from their work to silence the cacophonous cling-clang.
Plenty of pushing and shoving occurred in retaliation. Drinking fuelled the
rowdy behaviour of the onlookers and the marchers alike. The eighteenth-
century canon who summarized the manuscript describing the mêlée likened
the rowdy ritual to other carnivalesque practices of the medieval church, like
the Feast of Fools or the annual pretense of a boy bishop presiding at the cathedral. It was all good fun, except perhaps to men and women of Philippe of
Cahors's character. He appears not to have permitted the black procession
during his episcopate.

Throughout his career as bishop of Évreux, Philippe of Cahors was at the
disposal of the crown and, to a lesser extent, of other great men and institutions, especially in the capital. Why? First, he was a bishop in a strategic province. Absent this geopolitical reality, the other reason, namely, the renown of
his earlier career as an administrator and adviser to King Louis IX, would have
had less impact. Elite parties recruited him as a respected Christian to dignify
with his presence ceremonies in which they manifested their magnanimity or
self-worth more generally. Of course, he could choose among the events and
ceremonies to which he travelled and in which he participated, and scholars
can only guess at what sorts of events he declined to attend. Nonetheless, a
recounting, by no means exhaustive, of a few of the instances in which he
consented to be present or take part will give a flavour of these aspects of the
Cahorsin's career.

He stood up as a worthy witness in ceremonies like those in which lay lords
swore homage to churchmen. At least twice the churchman receiving the homage was Étienne Tempier, the bishop of Paris. The first was in 1268, before
Philippe was a bishop, and the occasion was the homage that the king's son
Jean, the count of Nevers, rendered to Étienne (discussed above with reference
to the simple title used to refer to him, though he was guard of the seal and considered chancellor). As bishop of Évreux, he also formally witnessed the count
of Bar's swearing of homage to the Parisian prelate on Tuesday, 10 November
1271.[173] Other ceremonies that saw him in attendance included the "proving" of
the authenticity of the relics of Saint Firmin in Amiens on 14 May 1279.

Stories told of Firmin, a Navarrese Christian and the first bishop of Pamplona, being beheaded early in the fourth century (25 September 303), but

---

173 Fisquet, *France pontificale*, 8:29.

accounts differed as to where the martyrdom took place, either in Pamplona or in Amiens, where the saint was alleged to have been travelling when the execution by Roman authorities occurred. At the turn of the sixth/seventh century a bishop of Amiens discovered the remains of a body he took to be Firmin's, translated it to an appropriate shrine, and the cult took root. Nonetheless, the authenticity of the relics was not universally acknowledged. Philippe of Cahors was selected to be part of the commission that verified the relics. He subscribed to the attestation, and he also assisted at a new translation of the holy man's body.[174]

To summarize: Philippe of Cahors worked steadily and strenuously for more than a decade to maintain and, in numerous ways, to improve conditions in the bishopric of Évreux. He took measures to secure his authority from the pope over the non-exempt monastic houses in the diocese and over all the secular clergy. Not much love was lost between him and the monastery of Saint-Taurin, with which he had some testy conflicts. In this, he was no different from many of his predecessors but he held his own. He enjoyed cordial relations with his cathedral chapter and generally amicable relations with other churchmen and nuns in the diocese, although on rare occasions he had to exercise his disciplinary jurisdiction. In litigation, he defended his church's rights vigorously, but he was not vindictive to those who challenged his or his institution's claims. He was gentle with *miserabiles personae*, like orphans, even when they wrongfully claimed rights under what he regarded as the baleful influence of unscrupulous relatives. He carried through and completed serious projects, initiated before his episcopacy, to improve the fabric of the cathedral and, in support of this effort, to restore the church's properties to his and his canons' immediate landlordship. He was, in other words, a very fine bishop, and he managed this accomplishment while also maintaining light ties to Paris through the occasional visit there during which time he resumed his seat in *Parlement* with his old colleagues, as he had done in the days of King Louis IX. The memory of the king loomed larger as Philippe's episcopate continued. It is to that issue that we should now address ourselves.

---

174 Le Brasseur, *Histoire civile et ecclésiastique du comté d'Évreux*, p. 201; Fisquet, *France pontificale*, 8:29.

4

THE PRELATE AND HIS HOLY MAN

In 1268, Louis IX and two of his sons visited Évreux. The visit coincided with the king's preparations for his last crusade, scheduled to depart Paris in the spring of 1270. While they were there, he made known his intention to found a Dominican friary in the city, one that would complement the Franciscan house already established there.[1] I have linked this promise with the visit in 1268, even though at least two other scholars refer it to a royal visit to the city on 19 October 1259. On the earlier occasion the king and again two of his sons, Louis and Philip, attended the consecration of the bishop-elect, Raoul Grosparmi, in the abbatial church of Saint-Taurin.[2] Raoul was another of those men of humble origin whom Louis IX lifted from obscurity to positions of power. He was a man who would be true to his lord to the end.[3] He had been on the king's first crusade and was serving him as keeper of the seal when he entered the ranks of the episcopate.[4] He would die in the sands of North Africa while accompanying the future saint on his last crusade.[5] Many other notables were also present at Raoul's installation in Évreux in 1259.[6] These included Archbishop Eudes Rigaud of Rouen, who would be the new bishop's ecclesiastical superior, and Simon, earl of Leicester and comte de Montfort, who was already a leader in the struggle taking place in England between Henry III and his barons. Simon

---

1 Chassant and Sauvage, *Histoire des évêques d'Évreux*, p. 76; Masson-de-Saint-Amand, *Suite des essais historiques et anecdotiques*, p. 49.
2 Montaubin, "Raoul Grosparmi," pp. 432–3; Debidour, *Essai sur l'histoire de l'abbaye bénédictine de Saint-Taurin*, p. 138.
3 Montaubin, "Raoul Grosparmi," pp. 418–20.
4 Montaubin, "Raoul Grosparmi," pp. 418, 423–31.
5 Montaubin, "Raoul Grosparmi," pp. 437–8.
6 Montaubin, "Raoul Grosparmi," p. 432; Debidour, *Essai sur l'histoire de l'abbaye bénédictine de Saint-Taurin*, p. 138.

subsequently emerged as the driving force and the barons' leader in the quest for government reform. At this point, however, no one thought of Simon, who admired Louis IX, as a rebel.[7]

One may explain the presence of a galaxy of such important personages in part by the imminence of the final negotiations for the Treaty of Paris. This was the sworn accord that formally ended the war that had broken out in 1202 between King John of England and Louis IX's grandfather, Philip Augustus, and had led to the French acquisition of vast stretches of territories in western France.[8] Eudes Rigaud was a participant all along in the negotiations for the treaty. As keeper of the royal seal and, therefore, holder of the office in France closest to that of the (vacant) chancellorship, Raoul Grosparmi participated as well. As Pascal Montaubin has written, "all of the realm's political and diplomatic business passed through his hands."[9] Simon, earl of Leicester and comte de Montfort, was an important voice on the English side.[10] Proxies ratified the treaty in October 1259, even though a few points remained unresolved.[11] The English king intended to depart Dover for Paris in November 1259, since he needed to be present for the resolution of the last issues (wrapped up on 3 December) and to attend the solemn publication of the treaty on 4 December.[12]

Yet if Louis IX made a public promise in Évreux at this time to found a Dominican friary, he did not follow through. This would be very uncharacteristic of him, especially since he was hardly lacking in disposable cash in the years after 1259. A French screed defaming Henry III, popular in the sense that a non-elite street performer penned it, referred to Louis IX as "the rich man of Paris" at the time of the treaty.[13] The king was not in any financial straits until he began to prepare for his second crusade in the late 1260s and to earmark all available resources to the coming war.[14] This fact raises the suspicion that Louis IX made his promise to endow a Dominican friary in Évreux during a visit there towards the end of his reign, when, because of the outflow of cash to recruit an army, navy, weapons of war, and supplies for the invasion planned for 1270, it was not expedient immediately to follow through.

---

7 Maddicott, *Simon de Montfort*, pp. 90–3; Hershey, "Justice and Bureaucracy," pp. 848–9.

8 Jordan, *Tale of Two Monasteries*, pp. 59–65.

9 Jordan, *Tale of Two Monasteries*, p. 62; Montaubin, "Raoul Grosparmi," p. 428.

10 Treharne, *Baronial Plan of Reform*, p. 141.

11 Chaplais, *Essays in Medieval Diplomacy*, Essay 1, "The Making of the Treaty of Paris (1259) and the Royal Style," pp. 238–47; Cuttino, *English Medieval Diplomacy*, p. 10.

12 Chaplais, *Essays in Medieval Diplomacy*: Essay 1, "The Making of the Treaty of Paris (1259) and the Royal Style," p. 238; Cuttino, *English Medieval Diplomacy*, p. 10.

13 Symes, *Common Stage*, p. 255.

14 Reitz, *Die Kreuzzüge Ludwigs*, 9:179–224.

This would also mean that the two sons who accompanied him on this latter visit were Philip and a sibling, but not Prince Louis, who had died soon after the publication in December 1259 of the Treaty of Paris. If the grief-stricken king had made a promise several weeks earlier in the presence of his beloved son, he would not have put off fulfilling it.[15] Multiple sources allude to the character of the sixteen-year-old boy and of his parents', especially his father's, love. Besides the sources I have adduced elsewhere,[16] Archbishop Eudes Rigaud himself testified to the king's affection for a son "marvelously endowed with grace and intelligence."[17] The epitaph prepared for the boy's tomb and recorded by Duchesne memorialized the sentiment, "a youth gracious to God and persons [and] ... adorned by the integrity of his character."[18] At the time his son took sick, indeed, I have argued that the king was considering having him crowned co-king in the tradition of Capetian succession practised from 987 to 1179. Already in the seventeenth century, learned students of the reign were coming to the same conclusion from their examination of the sources. Tillemont intimated that this was François Duchesne's opinion, but François may have been repeating what he had already learned from his father, the other great antiquary in the family, André Duchesne.[19]

Eudes Rigaud, who had been in Évreux in 1259, came to Paris in 1260 to comfort the king on the prince's death with wisdom drawn from the Bible, especially emphasizing the virtue in Job's bearing of his divine-sanctioned tribulations that included the deaths of his children. A fable the archbishop told about a titmouse who escaped a peasant's clutches and whose moral was the futility of recovering what one has lost also soothed the king's feelings. More to the point, Eudes's presence would also have brought the king's promise of building a friary, a vow to God, to the ruler's mind, *if he had made any such promise*.[20] That he assigned no funds to such a project seems to prove that there was no promise.

We are therefore on firmer ground in dating the king's promise to 1268, two years before his death on crusade in Tunis. Given this conclusion, it makes sense that King Philip III made good on his father's promise in 1273, after

---

15 For the king's hopes for his son and his inordinate grief at his death, see Jordan, *"Etiam reges,"* pp. 628–33.

16 Jordan, *"Etiam reges,"* pp. 628, 631–3.

17 *Récits d'un ménestrel de Reims*, p. 291.

18 *Historiae francorum scriptores*, 5:442, "Adolescens Deo et hominibus gratiosus ... honestate morum adornatus."

19 Cf. Tillemont, *Vie de saint Louis*, 5:215–16.

20 *Récits d'un ménestrel de Reims*, pp. 291–2.

royal resources recovered from the financial drain of the crusade.[21] Preliminary discussions led to a decision to build the convent on a lot that once served as the farmyard for the adjacent castle of Évreux.[22] The young king needed a local man to manage matters. He chose Philippe of Cahors, who brokered the agreements that made the construction possible.[23] The bishop reassured the local parish priest, who initially feared that the new foundation would compromise the rights of his church, Notre-Dame-de-la-Ronde.[24] Yielding on the construction of the friary per se, the priest also offered no objections to the erection of a bell tower and the laying out of a cemetery on the convent grounds.

Only a few conditions attached to the priest's concessions. The future community of friars was not to make worship services available to laypeople on Sundays in competition with those of the parish church. It was to make an annual payment to the parish of 6 l. *tournois*, presumably to compensate for unforeseen problems for the parish church from the presence of the new community. The friars promised not to have their church dedicated to the Virgin or Mary Magdalene, because these two saints already served as the patrons of the parish church and the cathedral. The parish church also had a chapel consecrated to Mary Magdalene. The parish priest and perhaps the bishop foresaw that oblations in honour of these saints might redirect offerings away from their churches to new altars dedicated to the two Marys at the Dominican church. All the parties sealed the final agreement on the Tuesday after Trinity Sunday (the first Sunday after Pentecost) in 1275, according to a vidimus of the act.[25]

In all respects, during the years of planning and construction the bishop of Évreux oversaw work at the convent. At the end, Philippe also consecrated the building and the cemetery.[26] Évreux's modern diocesan archivist and historian, Adolphe-André Porée, came to consider the bishop as virtually a founder himself.[27] He had good reason. Two of the most intimate councillors of Louis IX, Geoffroy of Beaulieu and Guillaume of Chartres, towards the end of their lives may have retired from public service and taken up residence in Évreux or at least visited the bishop. Indeed, as soon as they were livable, rooms could have

---

21 Guilmeth, *Notice historique sur la ville ... d'Évreux*, p. 26.

22 Masson-de-Saint-Amand, *Suite des essais historiques et anecdotiques*, p. 49.

23 On the matters summarized in this and the following paragraph, see *Inventaire sommaire des Archives départementales ... Eure ... série H*, p. 225; Porée, *Histoire des évêques d'Évreux*, pp. 76–7; Le Brasseur, *Histoire civile et ecclésiastique du comté d'Évreux*, p. 200.

24 AD: Eure, H 1173.

25 AD: Eure, H 1173.

26 Guilmeth, *Notice historique sur la ville ... d'Évreux*, p. 26; Masson-de-Saint-Amand, *Suite des essais historiques et anecdotiques*, p. 49; Porée, *Histoire des évêques d'Évreux*, pp. 76–7.

27 Porée, *Anciens livres liturgiques*, p. 19 no. 65.

been made available at the new Dominican friary there, maintaining, as it were, a small and perhaps changing circle, with Bishop Philippe, of admirers of the late king.[28] Geoffroy was an adviser to Louis IX before he became a Dominican.[29] After this, he served for two decades as the king's confessor. Both before and after the king's death, he associated himself with institutions that Louis IX favoured, preaching, for example, and supervising almsgiving at the king's foundation, the *Grand Béguinage* of Paris.[30] Geoffroy also accompanied the king on both of his crusades and died about 1276 or a little before, some authors think in Évreux.[31] Guillaume of Chartres, one of the king's chaplains and from the mid-1260s on a Dominican friar as well, also went on both crusades. He died between 1277 and 1280.[32] Both men recorded their memories of the king in biographies/hagiographies that they possibly wrote in Évreux.[33]

Initially dedicated to Saints Peter and Paul by the bishop, the Dominican church received a new dedication to the royal saint after Louis IX's canonization in 1297. The then bishop of Évreux, Mathieu of Les Essarts, presided at this rededication in 1299.[34] It was in fact the very first church dedicated to Saint Louis.[35] It possessed one of the saint's contact relics, a chalice kept in a large silver reliquary, inventoried, together with another depicting Our Lady of Mercies, on 30 August 1790 for sale by agents of the revolutionary government.[36] The grounds of the friary were also the site of numerous of the saint's miracles, twenty-five of which occurred in the wake of the rededication.[37] The friars expeditiously put in an order for the fabrication of a new convent seal that may be the first or at least one of the first three seals to use the saint's representation as an emblem. The Quinze-Vingts, the hospital for the blind that the king had founded in Paris, and the consulate of Pézenas, a town that Louis had taken

---

28 Masson-de-Saint-Amand, *Suite des essais historiques et anecdotiques*, p. 49.
29 On Geoffroy, see *Sanctity of Louis IX*, pp. 32–4; Le Brasseur, *Histoire civile et ecclésiastique du comté d'Évreux*, p. 202.
30 Stabler Miller, *Beguines*, p. 180 no. 6.
31 E.g., Le Pesant, "Miracles de saint Louis à Évreux," p. 41.
32 *Sanctity of Louis IX*, p. 34; Jordan, *Men at the Center*, pp. 17–18; Forcadet, "Les premiers juges de la Cour du roi," p. 227; Le Brasseur, *Histoire civile et ecclésiastique du comté d'Évreux*, p. 202.
33 Translations of their writings make up the bulk (pp. 69–172) of *Sanctity of Louis IX*.
34 *Opuscules et mélanges historiques sur la ville d'Évreux*, p. 67; Chassant and Sauvage, *Histoire des évêques d'Évreux*, p. 77; Le Brasseur, *Histoire civile et ecclésiastique du comté d' Évreux*, p. 201.
35 Avril, *Les archives héraldiques d'Évreux*, p. 74.
36 AD: Eure, H 1173, "Inventaire des Jascobins," fol. 10 v.
37 *Historiae francorum scriptores*, 5:477–80; Le Pesant, "Miracles de saint Louis à Évreux," p. 41.

under his protection in 1262 through the good offices of a branch of none other than Philippe of Cahors's family, fabricated the other two seals.[38]

At the opening of this book, I imagined the three elderly men, Philippe of Cahors, Geoffroy of Beaulieu, and Guillaume of Chartres, and perhaps other old friends, passing through Évreux, reminiscing about their time in the king's entourage. Perhaps they also talked theology. An inscription in a book-length collection of the letters of Saint Augustine asserts that the tome belonged to the confessor of Saint Louis, which would mean the Dominican friar Geoffroy of Beaulieu. Before being inscribed, the book "travelled" after the royal confessor's death. In the year 1324 a Dominican of Paris purchased it for the convent there, and it was he who inscribed it, "This was the book of the most pious confessor of Saint Louis, king of the Franks."[39] In the 1270s, Geoffroy, Guillaume, and Philippe were part of the remnant, rapidly declining in number, of those, as I said, dedicated like Louis IX to redemptive governance. When they were able, they attended the funerals of the like-minded disciples of the king, as Philippe did for the *prévôt* of Paris, Étienne Boileau. The miracles that Guillaume recorded and the record of Louis IX's holy deeds that he and Geoffroy preserved in their books testify to their expectation that the canonization was in the offing. Then, not long after he finished his biography, Geoffroy died. Within a year or two, again soon after he finished his book about the king, Guillaume also passed away. Philippe, bereft of his long-time friends, could only wonder at how the machinery of the church had delayed in honouring their old master.

Philippe was probably aware that his time on earth was rapidly diminishing. Motivated perhaps by the passing of his friends, he prepared for his own end. Around the year Guillaume of Chartres died, the bishop had his will drafted. It was none too soon to arrange things, as scrutiny of the record of events for the year 1281 reveals. The series of incidents that have brought me to make this statement indirectly concern the creation of a new parish in the diocese of Évreux that year. Ecclesiastical authorities occasionally combined adjacent parishes, the reader will recall, where population shifts made it impossible for one or both of the congregations to support a priest and the fabric of a church.

---

38 *Histoire générale du Languedoc*, 3:496; *Layettes*, *4*, no. 4750; Chassel, "De l'amour du prince au culte de saint Louis," pp. 65–8; Jordan, "Philippe of Cahors; Or, What's in a Name?"

39 Omont, Note from "Séance du Conseil d'administration," p. 163, "Fuit iste liber pusinii [*lisez:* piisimi] confessoris sancti Ludovici regis Francorum." An alternative translation would make it the king's book, but the usual word order in that case would place the word *confessoris* after *Ludovici*, not before *sancti*.

The reverse was also necessary where population had exploded or a community had grown up in a formerly unsettled area.[40] The latter proved to be the case in the Évrecin after some extensive assarting (*essarts, défrichements*) that took place in the forest of Neubourg.[41] The village, established during and in the wake of the clearance and aptly named La Neuville-du-Bosc (Newtown-out-of-the-Woodland), was to have its own church.[42] Dedicated to Saint Catherine, the planned edifice required a portion of the available tithes for long-term maintenance. The monks of the abbey of Bec-Hellouin, who sponsored the clearance, came to a preliminary understanding with Bishop Philippe on this unexpectedly complex matter, an understanding that, on reflection, proved unsatisfactory and required renegotiation.[43]

One would assume that the two prelates involved, the abbot of Bec, Pierre of La Chambrie, and Bishop Pierre, along with their legal advisers, would plan to meet and hammer out a modified agreement. Instead, the prelates delegated their authority to proctors. The abbot appointed a cleric, Richard Pelé, to act on his behalf. On 28 March 1281, Richard presented his credentials to the arbiter.[44] Later, on 5 May 1281, the bishop's proctor, Gérard of Antilly, also presented his.[45] The unusual five-week delay might not testify to any particularly intractable or even complex problems. Perhaps the arbiter, no less a man than the archbishop of Rouen, Gullaume (II) of Flavicourt,[46] was busy in Rouen or elsewhere on other business. The likelihood, however, given the length of the delay, is that the bishop of Évreux fell ill in March, the seasonal peak in influenza and pneumonia in France, judging from modern observation,[47] to which men of his age were susceptible, and that he could not attend to affairs. When he seemed to recover in early May, he went back to work and gave his formal approval to Gérard of Antilly's appointment as his proctor.[48] Yet it is clear from the record of this affirmation that Gérard had already been participating in negotiations without Philippe's formal authorization.

---

40 For additional examples, see *Les manuscrits classiques latins*, p. 305, especially no. 1; *Register of Eudes of Rouen*, p. 631; Morel, "La division de la ville de Compiègne en trois paroisses," pp. 253–5; Lachiver, *Histoire de Mantes*, pp. 66–8 no. 97.

41 AD: Eure, G 6, pp. 121–3.

42 AD: Eure, G 6, pp. 124–5. See also Porée, *Histoire de l'abbaye du Bec*, 1:623–4.

43 Inferred from AD: Eure, G 6, pp. 121–3.

44 AD: Eure, G 6, pp. 125–6.

45 AD: Eure, G 6, pp. 123–4.

46 AD: Eure, G 6, pp. 121–4.

47 Chowell, Miller, and Viboud, "Seasonal Influenza," https://www.ncbi.nlm.nih.gov/pmc/articles/PMC2680121/.

48 AD: Eure, G 6, pp. 123–4.

Indeed, under the watchful eye of the archbishop of Rouen, the two proctors had already reached a tentative accord before 5 May and were ready to submit a final draft for approval on 25 May.[49] Then there was another evidently unexpected delay, not as long as before, but unusual in the circumstances and again possibly attributable to Philippe of Cahors's continuing weak health. He was not present or perhaps could not be present when all the other parties involved approved the draft of the final protocols on 31 May 1281.[50] The bishop's circumstances once again delayed his personal approval for a couple of days until 2 June 1281.[51] The negotiations, from start to finish, extended over nearly half a year.

The bishop's end was imminent. People in Évreux may have suspected this, but people in Paris appear to have been unaware. Indeed, ignorant of circumstances in Évreux, King Philip III transmitted a request to Philippe of Cahors to join with two old comrades, Mathieu of Vendôme and Henri of Vézelay, to represent him in a dispute with Simon de Perruche, the bishop of Chartres, over the right to make several appointments in the Chartrain. Upon receiving the king's request, Philippe accepted the charge. Did he feel himself recovering? Did he expect to fully regain his stamina? The panel finished its work in late July, and a decision based on the negotiations was formally issued on 1 August 1281.[52] It was the last act in which Philippe of Cahors was a major participant in any way. Later in the same month, he died. The fullest transcription of his epitaph, to which we shall return, provides the precise date of 6 August, a date that the early historian Guillaume Lacoste accepted.[53] "[P]er semel M bis C, / [jungens] bis quater X, semel I luxit et Augusti bis / tertia funere justi" (one thousand once, one hundred twice / together with twice four decades, one once / light broke in on August twice the third [day] ...). Other partial transcriptions, partial because the epitaph was effaced over time, record the tumulary date slightly differently in small ways, or include *jungens* (Lacoste does not) or make the day of the month the twenty-first, as if the phrase "twice the third [day]" should be read "twice the third [week]."[54]

The tomb from which the earliest antiquaries copied the epitaph was not in the cathedral church. Philippe, it is not at all surprising, opted for interment in

---

49 Porée, *Histoire de l'abbaye du Bec*, 1:624.
50 AD: Eure, G 6, pp. 121–3.
51 Porée, *Histoire de l'abbaye du Bec*, 1:624–5.
52 Fisquet, *France pontificale*, 8:29–30.
53 Lacoste, *Histoire générale de la province de Quercy*, 2:350.
54 Fisquet, *France pontificale*, 8:30; Porée, *Sépultures des évêques d'Évreux*, p. 8; Le Brasseur, *Histoire civile et ecclésiastique du comté d'Évreux*, p. 202.

the middle of the choir of the Dominican church of Saints Peter and Paul in Évreux, founded by Louis IX, endowed by his son, and later dedicated to the canonized king.[55] This was the foundation whose construction he supervised and blessed at the time of its completion. This was the also the building or, rather, complex of buildings where for a brief time Guillaume of Chartres, Geoffroy of Beaulieu, and he may have reminisced about their former royal master. The tomb, however, has not survived. We can imagine its appearance from the sketch and description of the antiquary Roger de Gaigniêres, numbered 2366 in the present inventory of the Gaigniêres Collection. He described it as yellow copper with the effigy of the bishop in a Gothic framing ("dans un encadrement gothique").[56] A sketch of his evidently lost original, on a loose folio, migrated to England and is now in the Bodleian Library.[57] The inscription on the perimeter is distinctive in that it names the effigist "Guillaume de Plalli me facit" (Plailly, Oise).[58] Such personal ascriptions on medieval sculpture are exceedingly rare this early,[59] but not so rare as to make this example the first of its kind, an honour sometimes awarded it by British scholars. In some way – probably through a single faulty transcription, published and copied repeatedly in English-language encyclopedias, handbooks, and graphic collections of medieval and early modern stone and metal work – insular scholars have long dated the tomb effigy not to 1281 but to 1241.[60]

Aside from the intricate dating clauses cited and translated above, the epitaphist composed his memorial in simple Latin verse. The earliest attempted transcription occurs on the last folio of one of the ordinals of the burial church.[61] Ordinals, the liturgical books that churches maintained as guides to their various services, regularly needed updating as new feasts, altars, and rites came into being, but the preservation of superseded versions was common

---

55 Fisquet, *France pontificale*, 8:30; Porée, *Sépultures des évêques d'Évreux*, p. 8. In error, Forcadet, "Les premiers juges de la Cour du roi," p. 254, locates his burial in the Franciscan church (with the *Cordeliers*).

56 *Inventaire des dessins exécutés pour Roger de Gaigniêres*, 1:285 no. 2366.

57 Online at https://catalogue.bnf.fr/ark:/12148/cb40556528k. It serves as the cover art of this book. My thanks to Randall Pippenger for locating the sketch.

58 *Inventaire des dessins exécutés pour Roger de Gaigniêres*, 1:285 no. 2366; *Roger de Gaigniêres (1642–1715) – Collectionneur*, p. 144.

59 Mély, *Primitifs français et leurs signatures*, p. 62.

60 E.g., Parker, *Glossary of Terms*, pp. 253–4; Boutell, *Monumental Brasses and Slabs*, p. 164; Overall, Notice of a Paper on "Latten, Its History and Application," p. 572; Druitt, *Manual of Costume*, p. 14 no. 1.

61 Porée, *Anciens livres liturgiques*, p. 19 no. 65 (referring to Bibliothèque municipale de Rouen, MS 402); Porée, *Histoire des évêques d'Évreux*, p. 76; Avril, *Les archives héraldiques d'Évreux*, p. 74.

practice. They served for decades as (relevant) omnium-gatherums of local ecclesiastical traditions.[62] The Dominican ordinal of Évreux referred to above and dated to the fourteenth century was possibly the first commissioned after the canonization of Louis IX.[63] It was appropriate at the time to include information in it on Bishop Philippe, who saw to the execution of his royal friend's wishes. The book came into the hands of one of Bishop Philippe's successors, the early eighteenth-century prelate and bibliophile Jean Le Normand,[64] long after it had outlived its usefulness at the friary, and probably after Philippe's administrative role, of which nothing appears in the epitaph, had decisively faded from memory.

As with the dating formula, either the effaced character of the inscription or some other factor has caused the various transcriptions to differ slightly. The following is my best effort at reconciling the transcriptions.

> Continet haec fossa/Philippi praesulis ossa
> Quem precor, ad cetus/celestes collige, Christe;
> Nam pavit letus/in egenis saepe tuis te
> Hinc obitum disce/migrantis ad atria celi.[65]

(This grave contains the bones of Bishop Philippe, whom, I pray, O Christ, you bring to the heavenly assemblies. [With him] so often rejoicing in you, like one of your poor souls, make this death that of one who departs to the forecourts of heaven.)

The epitaph is conventional, as are the two words "funere justi" following the dating formula, quoted earlier, and thus the last phrase of the entire inscription.[66] Nevertheless, they sympathetically sum up the life of Philippe of Cahors in that they refer to his death as the moment for the eulogy or obsequies of a

---

62 Palazzo, *History of Liturgical Books*, pp. 221–8.
63 Porèe, *Anciens livres liturgiques*, p. 19 no. 6.
64 Porèe, *Anciens livres liturgiques*, p. 19 no. 6.
65 Chassant and Sauvage, *Histoire des évêques d'Évreux*, p. 76. These authors provide the fullest version of the epitaph I have found, although they omit a word, "jungens," attested in Lacoste's partial transcription, *Histoire générale de la province de Quercy*, 2:350. I have used the medieval forms *cetus*, *celestes*, and *celi*, although classicizing transcribers (like Chassant and Sauvage, loc. cit., and Porée, *Sépultures des évêques d'Évreux*, p. 9) reproduce these words as *coetus*, *coelestes*, and *coeli* or as *caetus*, *caelestes*, and *caeli*, indifferently. Clearly, there were no diphthongs in these words in the original inscription. See also Brasseur, *Histoire civile et ecclésiastique du comté d'Évreux*, p. 202.
66 Lacoste, *Histoire générale de la province de Quercy*, 2:350.

righteous man. This summation or judgment may resonate in another monument to him. Although not interred in the cathedral of Our Lady of Évreux, the bishop (and his episcopacy) received a *laudatio* in a window painting representing him that the cathedral chapter commissioned in his honour and had placed near one of the church's supporting columns ("Effigies dicti episcopi est depicta in tabello juxta pilleare").[67] Is this memorial proof merely of conventional pieties? Surely, more than this, for Philippe was a generous man. He had earned a handsome salary most of his adult life, especially while he was serving in high administrative offices (master of the King's Court and keeper of the seal). With his personal fortune, despite what he may have bestowed along the way as charity, he was in a position as he approached the end of his life to bequeath substantial movable property for the use of his successor bishops. In the bequest,[68] there were devotional and worship books, among them a breviary in two volumes, an antiphonary, a gradual, a missal with the gospels, epistles, and another text of the gradual according to the use of Paris. Also included in the gift were mitres, a pastoral staff (a gift to him from the archbishop of Rouen, Eudes Rigaud), a crozier, several bejewelled rings, and silver liturgical vessels. His successors and the scene they set would be impressive for the celebration of mass with the ministering bishops dressed in their pontificals and furnished with these accoutrements, as he had been. Cleverly, he left the safeguarding of the treasures to the chapter, and for its service he stipulated that each of his successor bishops had to support the canons' measures from their (the bishops') income. He augmented that income by providing a sum of money to invest in the expansion of episcopal properties.

Generosity, of course, perhaps especially at the point of death, is not the same as integrity. On this matter, a last piece of evidence is pertinent, though not conclusive. Julien Théry-Astruc has studied 570 cases of accusations and subsequent papal judicial inquiries and/or prosecutions of prelates in the long thirteenth century. These cases arose out of the popes' criminal jurisdiction over high churchmen. Théry-Astruc has identified 207 bishops who came under suspicion. It is probably true, as he has acknowledged, that a few cases have escaped his search, but it is nonetheless reassuring that Philippe of Cahors's name never appears in the data as a target of an accusation, let alone in an

---

67 "Ancien coutumier de l'église d'Évreux," p. 190; entry number 225 of the "Catalogue Gaignières, etc.," printed for the *Société libre d'agriculture, sciences, arts et belles lettres de l'Eure*, pp. 487–8, 490.

68 For a partial transcription of the will and related documents, see "Ancien coutumier de l'église d'Évreux," pp. 190–2 and the important notes. Le Brasseur, *Histoire civile et ecclésiastique du comté d'Évreux*, p. 203; Fisquet, *France pontificale*, 8:29.

investigation of him or trial. Moreover, none of the 220 abbots and abbesses accused in these cases was serving in the diocese of Évreux during Philippe's episcopate.[69] The evidence, as I intimated, is far from definitive, but at least it does not challenge the picture of the bishop's probity or the quality of his supervision of diocesan affairs.

If Philippe of Cahors died with any regret in late 1281, it may have been that he had not had an opportunity to testify at the canonization hearings for Louis IX that were scheduled for the upcoming spring at Saint-Denis. He may also have regretted as he neared death that he had not followed the example of his friends Geoffroy of Beaulieu and Guillaume of Chartres and written up his memories of the king. The information provided in such a book would have supplied far more explicit evidence of Philippe's self-perception, what he thought of his life and career – his own commentary on a life lived largely in public service – than I have been able to recover. What I have attempted is to tease out his character from the abundant administrative and judicial material that we do have – secular and ecclesiastical. Philippe of Cahors knew that he was a participant in a great experiment to reform government, both secular and ecclesiastical, in the spirit of many thirteenth-century radical purists, not least the king himself. He knew that, to borrow Gandhi's words, "Man becomes great exactly in the degree in which he works for the welfare of his fellow-men."[70] To most of his contemporaries, as far as one can tell, Philippe lived an exemplary life in his service to the crown and the church, and as Delisle once put it, there ought to be some merit in excavating the evidence on which they founded their judgment. One certainly hopes so.

---

69 Théry-Astruc, "Judicial Inquiry as an Instrument of Centralized Government," pp. 875–89; Théry-Astruc, "'Excès', 'affaires d'enquête' et gouvernement de l'Église (v. 1150–v. 1350)," pp. 164–236; and Théry-Astruc, email to author, 20 December 2016.
70 Gandhi, *A Day Book of Thoughts*, p. 101.

BIBLIOGRAPHY

PRIMARY SOURCES: MANUSCRIPT

I have consulted manuscripts in digital form, traditional photographs, and directly in various French collections, such as the Archives Départementales de l'Eure (AD: Eure) and the *RegeCart, regestes de cartulaires*, ed. IRHT – section de diplomatique. The titles/descriptions and shelf numbers of the individual manuscripts are provided in the notes.

PRIMARY SOURCES: PUBLISHED

Actes du Parlement de Paris. Edited by Edgar Boutaric. 2 vols. Paris: Henri Plon, 1863–7.

Alighieri, Dante. *Purgatorio*. Translated by Allen Mandelbaum. New York: Bantam, 1982.

Alighieri, Dante. *Purgatorio*. Translated by Jean Hollander and Robert Hollander. New York: Random House, 2003.

"Ancien coutumier de l'église cathédrale d'Évreux, vulgairement appelé 'Hunaud.'" Edited by François Blanquart. *Société de l'histoire de Normandie: Mélanges* 6 (1906): 37–202.

Archives administratives de la ville Reims. Edited by Pierre Varin. 3 vols. Paris: Crapelet, 1839–48.

"Attestation de Guillaume de Brosse, archevêque de Sens (1258–1269), concernant la justice exercée par le Chapitre de Sens sur les hommes 'levant et couchant,' à Soucy près Sens." Edited by Gustave Julliot, *Bulletin de la Société archéologique de Sens* 15 (1892): 64.

Cartulaire de l'église Notre Dame de Paris. Edited by Benjamin Géraud. 4 vols. Paris: Crapelet, 1850.

"Catalogue Gaignières, etc." *Recueil des travaux de la Société libre d'agriculture, sciences, arts et belles lettres de l'Eure*, 4th ser. 9 (1891): 485–90.

Chartrier de l'Abbaye-aux[-]Bois (1202–1341): Étude et édition. Edited by Brigitte Pipon. Paris: École des chartes, 1996.

Chartular von Saint-Nicaise in Reims (13. Jahrhundert): Eine Untersuchung des Sprachgebrauchs und des volkssprachlichen Einflusses. Edited by Karina Anne High. Diplomarbeit. University of Vienna, 2013.

Conciliorum oecumenicorum generaliumque decreta. Edited by Giuseppe Alberigo and Alberto Melloni. 3 vols. Turnhout: Brepols, 2006.

Confessions et jugements de criminels au Parlement de Paris (1319–1350). Edited by Monique Langlois and Yvonne Lawhers. Paris: S.E.V.P.E.N. 1971.

Correspondance administrative d'Alfonse de Poitiers. Edited by Auguste Molinier. 2 vols. Paris: Imprimerie nationale, 1894–1900.

"Early Norman Charters." In *Tabularia*, edited by Nicholas Vincent. In press.

Gallia christiana in provincias ecclesiasticas distributa. 16 vols. Paris: V. Palmé, etc., 1856–99.

Gandhi, Mohandas. *A Day Book of Thoughts.* Edited by K.T. Narasimhachar. Madras: Macmillan, 1969.

Guillaume of Chartres. See *The Sanctity of Louis IX.*

Historiae francorum scriptores. Edited by André and François Duchesne. 5 vols. Paris: S. Cramoisy, 1636–49.

Inventaire des dessins exécutés pour Roger de Gaignières et conservés aux Départements des estampes et des manuscripts. Vol. 1, compiled by Henri Bouchot. Paris: E. Plon, Nourrit et Cie., 1891.

Joinville, Jean de. *Vie de saint Louis.* Edited and translated by Jacques Monfrin. Paris: Garnier, 1995.

Langlois, Charles-Victor, ed. *Formulaires des lettres du XIIe, du XIIIe et du XIVe siècle.* Paris: Imprimerie nationale, 1890.

Langlois, Charles-Victor, ed. *Textes relatifs à l'histoire du Parlement depuis les origines jusque'en 1314.* Paris: Alphonse Picard, 1888.

Layettes du Trésor des chartes. Edited by Alexandre Teulet et al. 5 vols. Paris: H. Plon, 1863–1909.

"Majus chronicon lemovicense a Petro Coral et aliis conscriptum." In *Recueil des historiens des Gaules et de la France*, edited by Martin Bouquet et al., vol. 21, 761–88. Paris: V. Palmé, 1855.

Manuscrits classiques latins des bibliothèques publiques de France. Vol. 1, *Agen-Évreux*, compiled by Colette Jeudy and Yves-François Riou. Paris: Éditions du Centre national de la recherche scientifique. 1989.

"Martini oppaviensis Chronicon pontificum et imperatorum." In *Monumenta Germaniae Historica, Scriptorum*, edited by Ludwig Weiland, vol. 22, 377–475. Hanover: Hahn, 1872.

Olim, ou, Registres des arrêts rendus par la Cour du roi. Edited by Arthur Beugnot. 3 vols. Paris: Imprimerie royale, 1839–48.

Ordonnances des rois de France de la troisième race. Edited by Eusèbe-Jacques de Laurière et al. 21 vols. Paris: Imprimerie royale [impériale, nationale], 1723–1849.

Pierre de Fontaines. *Le Conseil de Pierre de Fontaines ou traité de l'ancienne jurisprudence française.* Edited by Ange Ignace Marnier. Paris: Durand et Joubert, 1846.

Pouillé du diocèse de Cahors. Edited by Auguste Longnon. Paris: Imprimerie nationale, 1877.

"Quelques chartes anciennes de la ville de Chauny." In *Comptes-rendus et mémoires du Comité archéologique de Noyon,* edited by Poissonnier, 253–326. 1882.

Récits d'un ménestrel de Reims. Translated by Marie-Geneviève Grossel. Valenciennes: Presses Universitaires de Valenciennes, 2002.

Recueil des historiens des Gaules et de la France. Edited by Martin Bouquet et al. 24 vols. Paris: V. Palmé, 1840–1904.

Regestrum visitationum Archiepiscopi Rothomagensis = Journal des visites pastorales d'Eudes Rigaud, archevêque de Rouen, 1248–1269, publié pour la première fois, d'après le manuscrit de la Bibliothèque nationale. Edited by Théodose Bonnin. Rouen: A. Le Brument, 1852.

Register of Eudes of Rouen. Translated by Sydney Brown. New York: Columbia University Press, 1964.

Roger de Gaignières (1642–1715) – Collectionneur. http://data.bnf.fr/documents-by -rdt/12115323/4030.

The Sanctity of Louis IX: Early Lives of Saint Louis by Geoffrey of Beaulieu and William of Chartres. Edited by M. Cecilia Gaposchkin and Sean Field, translated by Larry Field. Ithaca: Cornell University Press, 2014.

"Visites pastorales de maître Henri de Vezelai." Edited by Léopold Delisle. *Bibliothèque de l'École des chartes* 54 (1893): 457–66 and plate.

SECONDARY SOURCES

1212–1214: El trieno que hizo a Europa. Pamplona: Publicaciones del Gobierno de Navarra, 2011

Albe, Édmond. "Autour de Jean XXII: Jean XXII et les familles du Quercy (suite)." *Annales de Saint-Louis des Français* 7 (1902–3): 141–234.

Albe, Édmond. "Les marchands de Cahors à Londres au XIIIe siècle." *Bulletin de la Société des études littéraires, scientifiques et artistiques du Lot* 33 (1908): 31–55.

Albe, Édmond. "Prélats originaires du Quercy: diocèses de France." *Annales de Saint-Louis des Français* 10 (1905–6): 139–211.

Avril, Robert, vicomte de Burey. *Les archives héraldiques d'Évreux.* Évreux: Charles Hérissey, 1890.

Baldwin, John. *The Government of Philip Augustus*. Berkeley: University of California Press, 1986.

Baldwin, John. *Masters, Princes and Merchants: The Social Views of Peter the Chanter and His Circle*. 2 vols. Princeton: Princeton University Press, 1970.

Baldwin, John, and Walter Simons. "The Consequences of Bouvines." *French Historical Studies* 37 (2014): 243–69.

Baluze, Étienne. *Vitae paparum avenionensium*. 4 vols. Paris: Muguet, 1693.

Berthe, Maurice. "Les élites urbaines méridionales au moyen âge (XIe–XVe siècles)." In *Mémoires de la Société archéologique du Midi de la France, hors série* (2002): 21–40. http://www.societes-savantes-toulouse.asso.fr/samf/memoires/hrseri2002 /BERTHE.PDF.

Blanquart, François. "Cerfs et sangliers annuellement délivrés à l'évêque d'Évreux en vertu d'usages forestiers." *Bulletins de la Société de l'histoire de Normandie* 13 (1919–24): 260–72.

Blanquart, François. "Droits de coutume exercés en la forêt d'Évreux par le chapitre de la cathédrale." *Bulletins de la Société de l'histoire de Normandie* 13 (1919–24): 272–4.

Blot, Alfred. *Notice historique et descriptive sur Évreux et ses environs*. Évreux: E. Dieu, 1880.

Boisjoslin, Jean de. *À travers les rue de Cahors: Répertoire historique et alphabétique des voies de cette ville*. Bayac: Éditions du Roc de Bourzac, 1993.

Bolton, Brenda. "Ottobuono." In *Oxford Dictionary of National Biography*. http:// www.oxforddnb.com/view/article/50348.

Borel d'Hauterive, André [= André-François-Joseph Borel]. *Histoire des armoiries des villes de France*. http://www.euraldic.com/lasu/tx/txt_vbh_somm.html.

Borrelli de Serres, Léon-Louis. *Recherches sur divers services publics du XIIIe au XVIIe siècle*. 3 vols. Paris: A. Picard et fils, 1895–1909.

Bourassé, Jean-Jacques. *Touraine: Histoire et monuments*. Tours: Mame, 1855.

Boutaric, Edgar. "Review of Martin Bertrandy[-Lacabane], *Recherches historiques sur l'origine, l'élection at le couronnement du pape Jean XXII*." *Bibliothèque de l'École des chartes* 16 (1855): 61–2.

Boutell, Charles. *Heraldry, historical and popular*. 2nd ed. London: Winsor and Newton, 1863.

Boutell, Charles. *Monumental Brasses and Slabs: An Historical and Descriptive Notice ... of the Middle Ages*. London: G. Bell, 1847.

Brundage, James. *Law, Sex, and Christian Society in Medieval Europe*. Chicago: University of Chicago Press, 1987.

"Cahors." In *La grande encyclopédie, inventaire raisonné des sciences, des lettres, et des arts*. Vol. 8, pp. 769–70. Paris: H. Lamirault et Cie., and others, 1889.

Campbell, George. *The Civil Service in Britain*. 2nd ed. London: G. Duckworth, 1965.

Campbell, Gerard. "The Attitude of the Monarchy toward the Use of Ecclesiastical Censures in the Reign of Saint Louis." *Speculum* 35 (1960): 535–55.

Campbell, Gerard. "Temporal and Spiritual Regalia during the Reigns of St. Louis and Philip III." *Traditio* 20 (1964): 351–83.

Carolus-Barré, Louis. "Les Baillis de Philippe le Hardi." *Annuaire-Bulletin de la Société de l'histoire de France* (1966–7): 111–244.

Carolus-Barré, Louis, comp. *Le procès de canonisation de saint Louis (1272–1297): Essai de reconstitution*. Rome: École française de Rome, 1994.

Cathédrale Notre-Dame d'Évreux. Évreux: privately printed for the Cathedral of Évreux, n.d.

Challet, Vincent. "Marie Dejoux, *Les enquêtes de saint Louis: Gouverner et sauver son âme*." *Cahiers de recherches médiévales et humanistes* (2014). http://crm .revues.org/13291.

Chaplais, Pierre. *Essays in Medieval Diplomacy and Administration*. London: Hambledon, 1981.

Charon, Philippe. *Princes et principautés au moyen âge: L'exemple de la principauté d'Évreux, 1298–1412*. Paris: École des chartes, 2014.

Chassant, Alphonse, and G.-E. Sauvage. *Histoire des évêques d'Évreux avec des notes et des armoires*. Évreux: Louis Tavernier, 1846.

Chassel, Jean-Luc. "De l'amour du prince au culte de saint Louis: Le sceau des consuls de Pézenas (1298 ou 1303?)." In *Amour et desamour du prince du haut moyen âge à la Revolution française*, edited by Josiane Barbier, Monique Cottret, and Lydwine Scordia, 63–80. Paris: Éditions Kimé, 2011.

Châtelain, Émile. "Notes sur quelques tavernes fréquentées par l'Université de Paris aux XIV et XVe siècles." *Bulletin de la Société de l'histoire de Paris et de l'Ile de France* 25 (1898): 87–109.

Cheyette, Frederic. "The Royal Safeguard in Medieval France." *Studia Gratiana* 15 (1972): 631–52.

Chiffoleau, Jacques. "Saint Louis, Frédéric II et les constructions institutuionelles du XIIIe siècle." *Médiévales* 34 (1998): 13–23.

Chowell, G., M.A. Miller, and C. Viboud. "Seasonal Influenza in the United States, France, and Australia: Transmission and Prospects for Control." *Epidemiology and Infection* 136 (2008). https://www.ncbi.nlm.nih.gov/pmc/articles/PMC2680121/.

Claverie, Pierre-Vincent. "Un exemple de transfert logistique lié à la défense de la Terre sainte: Le passage en Orient de Guillaume de Roussillon (1275)." In *Migrations et diasporas méditerranéennes (Xe–XVIe siècles)*, edited by Michel Balard and Alain Ducellier, 475–83. Publications de la Sorbonne. https://books .openedition.org/psorbonne/6236?lang=en.

Cooke, William. "Menges." With an addendum by Richard Charnock. *Notes and Queries*, 7th ser. 4 (1887): 436.

Coquelle, Pierre. "Les clochers romans du Vexin Français et du Pincerais." *Mémoires de la Société historique et archéologique de l'arrondissement de Pontoise et du Vexin* 25 (1903): 47–65.

Corning, Caitlin. *The Celtic and Roman Traditions: Conflict and Consensus in the Early Medieval Church*. New York: Palgrave Macmillan, 2006.

Croix, Guillaume de la. *Histoire des évêques de Cahors*. Trans. Louis Ayma. 2 vols. Cahors: J.-G. Plantade, 1878–9.

Cuttino, George. *English Medieval Diplomacy*. Bloomington: Indiana University Press, 1985. data.bnf.fr. (online databank of the Bibliothèque nationale de France).

Davis, Adam. *The Holy Bureaucrat: Eudes Rigaud and Religious Reform in Thirteenth-Century Normandy*. Ithaca: Cornell University Press, 2006.

Debidour, Louis. *Essai sur l'histoire de l'abbaye bénédictine de Saint-Taurin jusqu'au XIVe siècle*. Évreux: C. Hérissey et fils, 1908.

Dejoux, Marie. "Gouverner par l'enquête en France de Philippe Auguste aux derniers Capétiens." *French Historical Studies* 37 (2014): 27–302.

Dejoux, Marie. *Les enquêtes de saint Louis: Gouverner et sauver son âme*. Paris: Presses Universitaires de France, 2014.

Delisle, Léopold. "Chronologie des baillis et des sénéchaux." In *Recueil des historiens des Gaules et de la France*, edited by Martin Bouquet et al., vol. 24, 15*–270*. Paris: V. Palmé, 1904.

Delisle, Léopold. "Notice sur vingt manuscrits du Vatican." *Bibliothèque de l'École des chartes* 37 (1876): 471–527.

Dictionnaire de droit canonique et des sciences en connexion avec le droit canon. Edited by J. Wagner. 3 vols. Paris: Hippolyte Walzer, 1894.

Dictionnaire de pédagogie et d'instruction primaire. Compiled by Ferdinand Buisson. 2 parts in 3 vols. Paris: Hachette, 1882–7.

Dictionnaire topographique du département de l'Aisne. Edited by Auguste Matton. Paris: Imprimerie nationale, 1871.

Dictionnaire topographique du département de l'Aube. Edited by Théophile Boutiot and Émile Socard. Paris: Imprimerie nationale, 1874.

Druitt, Herbert. *A Manual of Costume as Illustrated by Monumental Brasses*. London: De La More Press, 1906.

Église et état, église ou état? Les clercs et la genèse de l'état moderne. Edited by Christine Barralis, Jean-Patrice Boudet, Fabrice Delivré and Jean-Philippe Genet. Paris and Rome: Publications de la Sorbonne/École française de Rome, 2014.

Emanuel, Simcha. "Halakhic Questions of Thirteenth-Century Acre Scholars as a Historical Source." *Crusades* 17 (2018): 115–30.

Evergates, Theodore. *Marie of France: Countess of Champagne, 1145–1198*. Philadelphia: University of Pennsylvania Press, 2019.

Farmer, Sharon. *The Silk Industries of Medieval Paris: Artisanal Migration, Technological Innovation, and Gendered Experience*. Philadelphia: University of Pennsylvania Press, 2017.

Fawtier, Robert. *The Capetian Kings of France: Monarchy and Nation, 987–1328*. Translated by Lionel Butler and R.J. Adam. New York: St Martin's Press, 1960.

Félibien, Michel. *Histoire de la ville de Paris*. 5 vols. Paris: G. Desprez et J. Desessartz, 1725.

Fesler, James. "French Field Administration: The Beginnings." *Comparative Studies in Society and History* 5 (1962): 76–111.

Field, Sean. *Courting Sanctity: Holy Women and the Capetians*. Ithaca: Cornell University Press, 2019.

Fisquet, Honoré. *La France pontificale (Gallia christiana): Histoire chronologique et biographique des archevêques et évêques de tous les diocèses de France. Métropole de Rouen, Évreux*. Paris: E. Repos, 1866.

Flammermont, Jules. *Histoire des institutions municipales de Senlis*. Paris: F. Vieweg, 1881.

Föller, Carola. *Königskinder: Erziehung am Hof Ludwigs IX. des Heiligen von Frankreich*. Vienna, Cologne, and Weimar: Böhlau, 2018.

Forcadet, Pierre-Anne. "Les premiers juges de la Cour du roi au XIII siècle." *Revue historique de droit français et étranger* 94 (2016): 189–273.

Fossey, Jules. *Monographie de la cathédrale d'Évreux*. Évreux: Imprimerie de l'Eure, 1898.

Fournier, Paul. *Les officialités au moyen âge: Étude sur l'organisation, la compétence et la procédure des tribunaux ecclésiastiques ordinaires en France, de 1180 à 1328*. Paris: E. Plon, 1880.

Frowein, Peter. "Der Episkopat auf dem 2. Konzil von Lyon (1274)." *Annuarium historiae conciliorum* 6 (1974): 307–31.

Fulton Brown, Rachel. *Mary and the Art of Prayer: The Hours of the Virgin in Medieval Christian Life and Thought*. New York: Columbia University Press, 2018.

Gash, Norman. *Aristocracy and People: Britain, 1815–1865*. Cambridge, MA: Harvard University Press, 1979.

Goetzmann de Thune, Louis. *Essais historiques sur le sacre et couronnement des rois de France*. Paris: Vente, 1775.

Golb, Norman. *Les Juifs de Rouen au moyen âge: Portrait d'une culture oubliée*. Rouen: Publications de l'Université de Rouen, 1985.

Grandmottet, Odile. "Les officialités de Reims." *Bulletin d'information de l'Institut de Recherche et d'Histoire des Textes* 4 (1956): 77–106.

Grant, Lindy. *Architecture and Society in Normandy, 1120–1270*. New Haven: Yale University Press, 2005.

Grant, Lindy. *Blanche of Castile, Queen of France*. New Haven: Yale University Press, 2016.

Griffiths, Quentin. "The Capetian Kings and St. Martin of Tours." *Studies in Medieval and Renaissance History*, n.s. 9 (1987): 83–133.

Griffiths, Quentin. "Les origines et la carrière de Pierre de Fontaines, jurisconsulte de saint Louis: Une reconsidération avec documents inédits." *Revue historique de droit français et étranger*, 4th ser. 48 (1970): 544–67.

Griffiths, Quentin. "New Men among the Lay Counselors of Saint Louis' *Parlement*." *Mediaeval Studies* 32 (1970): 234–72.

Griffiths, Quentin. "St. Louis and the New Clerks of *Parlement*." *Studies in Medieval Culture* 4 (1974): 269–89.

Grunwald, Kurt. "Lombards, Cahorsins and Jews." *Journal of European Economic History* 4 (1975): 393–8.

Guilmeth, Alexandre-Auguste. *Notice historique sur la ville et les environs d'Évreux*. Rouen: A. Le Brument, 1849.

Hahn, Cynthia. *Strange Beauty: Issues in the Making and Meaning of Reliquaries, 400–circa 1204*. University Park: Pennsylvania State University Press, 2012.

Halperin, John. "Fiction That Is True: Trollope and Politics." In *The Trollope Critics*, edited by N. John Hall, 179–95. London: Macmillan, 1981.

Hélary, Xavier. *La dernière croisade: Saint Louis à Tunis (1270)*. Paris: Perrin, 2016.

Hélary, Xavier. "Pierre de la Broce, seigneur féodal et le service militaire sous Philippe III: L'ost de Sauveterre (1276)." *Journal des savants* 2 (2006): 275–305.

Hershey, Andrew. "Justice and Bureaucracy: The English Royal Writ and '1258.'" *English Historical Review* 113 (1998): 829–51.

Histoire générale du Languedoc. Edited by Joseph Vaissète and Claude Devic. 2nd ed. 16 vols. Edited by Auguste Molinier. Toulouse: E. Privat, 1872–1904.

Inventaire sommaire des Archives départementales antérieures à 1790: Eure, archives ecclésiastiques – série G. Edited by Georges Bourbon. Évreux: Imprimerie de Charles Hérissey, 1886.

Inventaire sommaire des Archives départementales antérieures à 1790: Eure, archives ecclésiastiques – série H. Edited by Georges Bourbon. Évreux: Imprimerie de Charles Hérissey, 1893.

Johnson, Penelope. *Equal in Monastic Profession: Religious Women in Medieval France*. Chicago: University of Chicago Press, 1991.

Jones, Andrew. *Before Church and State: A Study of Social Order in the Sacramental Kingdom of St. Louis IX*. Steubenville: Emmaus Academic, 2017.

Jordan, William. *The Apple of His Eye: Converts from Islam in the Reign of Louis IX.*
Princeton: Princeton University Press, 2019.

Jordan, William. "Christian Excommunication of Jews in the Middle Ages: A
Restatement of the Issues." *Jewish History* 1 (1986): 31–8.

Jordan, William. "The Cistercian Nunnery of La Cour Notre-Dame de Michery."
Revue bénédictine 95 (1985): 311–20.

Jordan, William. "*Etiam reges*, Even Kings." *Speculum* 90 (2015): 613–34.

Jordan, William. "Excommunication by Christian Authority." In *Medieval Jewish
Civilization: An Encyclopedia*, edited by Norman Roth. 245. New York: Routledge,
2003.

Jordan, William. *The French Monarchy and the Jews from Philip Augustus to the Last
Capetians.* Philadelphia: University of Pennsylvania Press, 1989.

Jordan, William. *Louis IX and the Challenge of the Crusade: A Study in Rulership.*
Princeton: Princeton University Press, 1979.

Jordan, William. *Men at the Center: Redemptive Governance under Louis IX.*
Budapest: Central European University Press, 2012.

Jordan, William. "Philippe of Cahors; Or, What's in a Name?" In *Festschrift for
Elizabeth A.R. Brown* (tentative title), edited by Cecilia Gaposchkin and Jay
Rubenstein. Forthcoming.

Jordan, William. "Review of Norman Golb, *The Jews in Medieval Normandy: A
Social and Intellectual History.*" *Jewish Quarterly Review* 89 (1999): 437–8.

Jordan, William. "Rustics Petitioning to *Parlement* in the Thirteenth Century: A Case
Study." *Haskins Society Journal,* forthcoming.

Jordan, William. "The Struggle for Influence at the Court of Philip III: Pierre de la
Broce and the French Aristocracy." *French Historical Studies* 24 (2001): 439–68.

Jordan, William. *A Tale of Two Monasteries: Westminster and Saint-Denis in the
Thirteenth Century.* Princeton: Princeton University Press, 2009.

Jordan, William. *Unceasing Strife, Unending Fear: Jacques de Thérines and the
Freedom of the Church in the Age of the Last Capetians.* Princeton: Princeton
University Press, 2005.

Jullien de Pommerol, Marie-Henriette, and Jacques Monfrin. "Les archives des
universités médiévales, problèmes de documentation." *Revue française de
pédagogie* 27 (1974): 6–21.

Kantorowicz, Ernst. *The King's Two Bodies: A Study in Mediaeval Political Theology.*
Princeton: Princeton University Press, 1957.

Kay, Richard. "An Episcopal Petition from the Province of Rouen, 1281." *Church
History* 34 (1965): 294–305.

Kibre, Pearl. *The Nations in the Medieval Universities.* Cambridge, MA: Medieval
Academy of America, 1948.

Lachiver, Marcel. *Histoire de Mantes et du Mantois à travers chroniques et mémoires.* Meulan: self-published, 1971.

Lacoste, Guillaume. *Histoire générale de la province de Quercy.* 4 vols. Cahors: Grime, 1883–6.

La grande encyclopédie: Histoire générale du Languedoc. 31 vols. Paris: H. Lamirault, 1886–1902.

Lannette, Claude. *Guide des Archives de l'Eure.* Évreux: [Archives départementales de l'Eure?], 1982.

Le Brasseur, Pierre. *Histoire civile et ecclésiastique du comté d'Évreux.* Paris: François Barois, 1722.

Lecanu, Auguste. *Histoire du diocèse de Coutances et Avranches.* 2 vols. Paris: Champion, 1877, and Rouen: Métérie, 1877.

Le Goff, Jacques. *Saint Louis.* Paris: Gallimard, 1996.

Le Pesant, Michel. "Les miracles de saint Louis à Évreux." *Nouvelles de l'Eure* 6 (October 1960): 41.

Maddicott, John. *Simon de Montfort.* Cambridge: Cambridge University Press, 1994.

Marquette, Jean-Bernard. "Pouvoir ecclésiastique et espace urbain." In *Des hommes et des pouvoirs dans la ville, XIVe–XXe siècles,* edited by Josette Pontet, 17–32. Bordeaux: Cesurb Histoire, 1999.

Mas Latrie, Louis de. *Trésor de chronologie, d'histoire et de géographie pour l'étude et l'emploi des documents du moyen-âge.* Paris: V. Palmé, 1889.

Masson[-de-]Saint-Amand, Armand-Narcisse. *Suite des essais historiques et anecdotiques sur le comté, les comtes, la ville d'Évreux et pays circonvoisins.* Évreux: Ancelle fils, 1815.

Massoni, Anne. "Les collégiales royales, ducales et comtales: Des institutions de fonctionnaires?" In *Église et état, église ou état? Les clercs et la genèse de l'état modern,* edited by Christine Barralis, Jean-Patrice Boudet, Fabrice Delivré, and Jean-Philippe Genet, 37–9. Paris and Rome: Publications de la Sorbonne/École française de Rome, 2014.

Mathisen, Ralph. "Desiderius of Cahors: Last of the Romans." In *Gallien in Spätantike und Frühmittelalter. Kulturgeschichte einer Region,* edited by S. Diefenbach and G. Müller, 455–69. Berlin: de Gruyter, 2013. https://www.academia.edu/11163235 /_Desiderius_of_Cahors_Last_of_the_Romans_.

Maudit, François-Joseph. *Histoire d'Ivry-la-Bataille et de l'abbaye de Notre-Dame d'Ivry.* Évreux: C. Hérissey, 1899.

Mély, Fernand. *Les primitifs français et leur signatures: Les sculptures.* Paris: L'Ami des monuments et des arts, 1908.

Mémoires et notes de M. Auguste Le Prévost pour servir à l'histoire du département de l'Eure. Edited by Léopold Delisle and Louis Passy. 2 vols. Évreux: A. Hérissey, 1862–9.

Menes, Valérie. "Les premiers acteurs de la vie parlementaire en France: Les légistes du Parlement de Paris (1254–1278)." In *Actes du 57e congrès de la CIHAE: Assemblées et parlements dans le monde, du moyen-âge à nos jours / Proceedings of the 57th ICHRPI Conference: Representative and Parliamentary Institutions in the World, from Middle Ages to Present Times*, edited by Jean Garrigues et al., 155–67. Paris: Assemblée nationale, 2010.

Mien-Péon, I.-P. *Le canton de Rozoy-sur-Serre*. Saint-Quentin: Jules Moreau, 1865.

Molinier, Auguste. "Catalogue des actes de Simon et d'Amauri de Montfort." *Bibliothèque de l'École des chartes* 34 (1873): 150–203 and 445–501.

Montaubin, Pascal. "Raoul Grosparmi, l'intime normand de saint Louis (années 1254–1262)." *Cahier des annales de Normandie* 35 (2009): 417–38.

Morel, Émile. "La division de la ville de Compiègne en trois paroisses en 1199." *Bulletin de la Société historique de Compiègne* 9 (1899): 253–5.

Nahon, Gérard. "Les juifs en Normandie au moyen âge." In *Nicolas de Lyre, franciscain de XIVe siècle, exégète et théologien*, edited by Gilbert Dahan, 29–50. Paris: Institut d'Études augustiniennes, 2011.

Nahon, Gérard. "Orality and Literacy: The French Tosaphists." In *Jews, Christians and Muslims in Medieval and Early Modern Times: A Festschrift in Honor of Mark R. Cohen*, edited by Arnold Franklin, Roxani Eleni Margariti, Marina Rustow, and Uriel Simonsohn, 145–68. Leiden: Brill, 2014.

Newman, William. *Les Seigneurs de Nesle en Picardie (XIIe–XIIIe siècle): Leurs chartes et leur histoire*. 2 vols. Paris: A. et J. Picard, 1971.

Nowacka, Keiko. "Persecution, Marginalization, or Tolerance: Prostitutes in Thirteenth-Century Parisian Society." In *Difference and Identity in Francia and Medieval France*, edited by Meredith Cohen and Justine Firnhaber-Baker, 175–96. Farnham: Ashgate, 2010.

Omont, Henri. Note from "Séance du Conseil d'administration." *Bulletin de la Société de l'histoire de Paris et de l'Ile de France* 16 (1889): 162–3.

Opuscules et mélanges historiques sur la ville d'Évreux et le département de l'Eure. Évreux: Jules Ancelle, 1845.

O'Toole, Barry. *The Ideal of Public Service: Reflections on the Higher Civil Service in Britain*. London: Routledge, 2006.

Overall, William. Notice of a Paper on "Latten, Its History and Application." *Transactions of the London and Middlesex Archaeological Society* 3 (1870): 572.

Palazzo, Eric. *A History of Liturgical Books from the Beginning to the Thirteenth Century*. Translated by Madeleine Beaumont. Collegeville: Liturgical Press, 1998.

"Papal Elections." *American Ecclesiastical Review* 5 (1891): 415–36.

Park, Danielle. *Papal Protection and the Crusader: Flanders, Champagne, and the Kingdom of France, 1095–1222*. Woodbridge: Boydell, 2018.

Parker, John. *A Glossary of Terms Used in Grecian, Roman, Italian, and Gothic Architecture*. Oxford: John Henry Parker, 1840.

Perrichet, Lucien. *La grande chancellerie de France des origines à 1328*. Paris: Recueil Sirey, 1912.

Pitoiset, Étienne. "Recherches sur les rues d'Évreux." *Recueil des travaux de la Société libre d'agriculture, sciences, arts et belles lettres de l'Eure*, 7th ser. 8 (1920): 93–195.

Pollock, Frederick, and Frederic Maitland. *The History of English Law before the Time of Edward I*. 2nd ed. 2 vols. Cambridge: Cambridge University Press, 1898.

Popkin, Jeremy. "Journals: The New Face of News." In *Revolution in Print: The Press in France, 1775–1800*, edited by Robert Darnton and Daniel Roche, 141–64. Berkeley: University of California Press, 1989.

Porée, Adolphe-André. *Histoire de l'abbaye du Bec*. 2 vols. Évreux: Charles Hérissey, 1901.

Porée, Adolphe-André. *Histoire des évêques d'Évreux*. Évreux: Louis Tavernier, 1846.

Porée, Adolphe-André. *Les anciens livres liturgiques du diocèse d'Évreux: Essai bibliographique*. Évreux: Imprimerie d'Eure, 1904.

Porée, Adolphe-André. *Sépultures des évêques d'Évreux*. Caen: Henri Delesques, 1891.

Powicke, Frederick (later Sir Maurice). *The Loss of Normandy, 1189–1204: Studies in the History of the Angevin Empire*. 2nd ed. Manchester: Manchester University Press, 1961.

Prochaska, F.K. *Women and Philanthropy in Nineteenth-Century England*. Oxford: Clarendon Press, 1980.

Rashdall, Hastings. *The Universities of Europe in the Middle Ages*. Edited by F.M. Powicke and A.B. Emden. 3 vols. Oxford: Oxford University Press, 1936.

Reitz, Dirk. *Die Kreuzzüge Ludwigs. IX von Frankreich 1248/1270*. Münster: LIT, 2005.

Renna, Thomas, "Church, Latin: Organization." In *Dictionary of the Middle Ages*, vol. 3, 372–7. New York: Charles Scribner's Sons, 1984.

Richard, Jean. "Les Conseillers de saint Louis, des grands barons aux premiers legists: Au point de recontre de deux droits." In *A l'ombre du pouvoir: Les Entourages princiers au Moyen Age*, edited by A. Marchandisse and J.-L. Kupper, 136–47. Geneva: Bibliothèque de la Faculté de philosophie et lettres de l'Université de Liege, 2003.

Richard, Jean. *Saint Louis: Roi d'une France féodale, soutien de la Terre sainte*. Paris: Fayard, 1983.

Rivière, Armand. *Histoire des biens communaux en France: Depuis leur origine jusqu'à la fin du XIIIe siècle*. Paris: Auguste Durand, 1856.

Savants et croyants: Les juifs d'Europe du Nord au moyen âge. Compiled by Nicolas Hatot and Judith Olszowy-Schlanger. Rouen and Ghent: Métropole Rouen Normandie and Snoek, 2018.

Schöpp, Natalie. *Papst Hadrian V.: Kardinal Ottobuono Fieschi.* Heidelberg: Carl Wintersbuchhandlung, 1916.

Schwarzfuchs, Simon. "Le vendredi 13 juin 1242: Le jour où le Talmud fut brûlé à Paris." *Revue des études juives* 173 (2014): 365–9.

"Session." *Académie des Inscriptions et Belles Lettres: Comptes rendus* (27 June 1980): 474.

Shatzmiller, Joseph. "Christian 'Excommunication' of the Jews: Some Further Clarifications." In *Shlomo Simonsohn Jubilee Volume: Studies on the History of the Jews in the Middle Ages and Renaissance Period,* 245–55. Tel Aviv: Tel Aviv University, Faculty of Humanities, Chaim Rosenberg School of Jewish Studies, 1993.

Shaul, Hollis. "The Prince and the Priors: Carthusian Monasticism and the Experience of State-Building in Angevin Provence, 1245–1385." PhD diss., Princeton University, 2018.

Sivéry, Gérard. *L'économie du royaume de France au siècle de saint Louis (vers 1180–vers 1315).* Lille: Presses Universitaires de Lille, 1984.

Stabler Miller, Tanya. *Beguines of Medieval Paris: Gender, Patronage, and Spiritual Authority.* Philadelphia: University of Pennsylvania Press, 2014.

Sullivan, Ceri. *Literature in the Public Service: Sublime Bureaucracy.* Basingstoke: Palgrave Macmillan, 2013.

Symes, Carol. *A Common Stage: Theater and Public Life in Medieval Arras.* Ithaca: Cornell University Press, 2007.

Tanon, Louis. *Histoire des justices des anciens églises et communautés monastiques de Paris.* Paris: L. Larose and Forcel, 1883.

Taylor, Antony. *Hostility to Aristocracy in Late Nineteenth- and Early Twentieth-Century Britain.* Basingstoke: Palgrave Macmillan, 2004.

Théry-Astruc, Julien. "'Excès,' 'affaires d'enquête' et gouvernement de l'Église (v. 1150–v. 1350): Les procédures de la papauté contre les prélats 'criminels,' première approche." In *Pathologie du pouvoir: Vices, crimes et délits des gouvernants (Antiquité, Moyen Âge, époque moderne),* edited by Patrick Gilli, 164–236. Leiden: Brill, 2016.

Théry-Astruc, Julien. "Judicial Inquiry as an Instrument of Centralized Government: The Papacy's Criminal Proceedings against Prelates in the Age of Theocracy (Mid-Twelfth to Mid-Fourteenth Century)." In *Proceedings of the Fourteenth International Congress of Medieval Canon Law,* edited by Joseph Goering, Stephan Dusil, and Andreas Thier, 875–89. Vatican City: Biblioteca Apostolica Vaticana, 2016.

Tillemont, Louis-Sébastien Le Nain de. *Vie de saint Louis, roi de France*. Edited by
J. de Gaulle. 6 vols. Paris: J. Renouard, 1847–51.

Treharne, R.F. *The Baronial Plan of Reform, 1258–1263*. Manchester: Manchester
University Press, 1971.

Turner, Dawson. *Account of a Tour in Normandy; Undertaken Chiefly for the Purpose
of Investigating the Architectural Antiquities of the Duchy, with Observations on
Its History, on the Country, and on Its Inhabitants*. 2 vols. London: J. and A. Arch,
1820.

Verger, Jacques. *Culture, enseignement et société en Occident aux XIIe et XIIIe
siècles*. Rennes: Presses Universitaires de Rennes, 1999.

Viard, Paul. *Histoire de la dîme ecclésiastique dans le royaume de France aux XII et
XIII siècles (1150–1313)*. Paris: A. Picard, 1912.

Watt, John. "The Papacy." In *The New Cambridge Medieval History*, vol. 5, edited by
David Abulafia, 107–63. Cambridge: Cambridge University Press, 1999.

Willemsen, Annemarieke. *Back to the Schoolyard: The Daily Practice of Medieval
and Renaissance Education*. Turnhout: Brepols, 2008.

Young, Spencer. *Scholarly Community at the Early University of Paris: Theologians,
Education and Society, 1215–1248*. Cambridge: Cambridge University Press, 2014.

INDEX

Printed and bound by CPI Group (UK) Ltd, Croydon, CR0 4YY

13/04/2025

14656517-0004